DIY
Sex & Relationship Therapy

Other personal development titles from How To Books:

CHALLENGING DEPRESSION AND DESPAIR
A medication-free, self-help programme that will change your life
Angela Patmore

88 CHINESE MEDICINE SECRETS
How to cultivate lifelong health, wisdom and happiness
Angela Hicks

FREE YOURSELF FROM ANXIETY
A self-help guide to overcoming anxiety disorders
Emma Fletcher and Martha Langley

EXPLORING YOUR DREAMS
How to use dreams for personal growth and creative inspiration
Ruth Snowden

Write or phone for a catalogue to:

How To Books
Spring Hill House
Spring hill Road
Begbroke
Oxford
OX5 1RX
Tel. 01865 375794

Or email: **info@howtobooks.co.uk**

Vist our website **www.howtobooks.co.uk** to find out more about us and our books.

Like our Facebook page **How To Books & Spring Hill**

Follow us on **Twitter @Howtobooksltd**

Read our books online **www.howto.co.uk**

DIY
Sex & Relationship Therapy

An effective self-help programme
for couples wanting to improve
their relationship

Dr Lori Boul with Dr June Kerr

howtobooks

Published by How To Books Ltd,
Spring Hill House, Spring Hill Road,
Begbroke, Oxford OX5 1RX, United Kingdom
Tel: (01865) 375794, Fax: (01865) 379162
info@howtobooks.co.uk
www.howtobooks.co.uk

How To Books greatly reduce the carbon footprint of their books by sourcing
their typesetting and printing in the UK.

British Library Cataloguing in Publication Data
A catalogue record for this book is available from the British Library

ISBN 978 1 84528 474 9

Cover design by Baseline Arts Ltd, Oxford
Produced for How To Books by Deer Park Productions, Tavistock
Typeset by Pantek Media, Maidstone, Kent
Printed and bound in Great Britain by Bell & Bain Ltd, Glasgow

Contents

Foreword

Sexual difficulties and problems are common in couples with relationship difficulties but not inevitable. Sex may be the sole means of communication that remains between a couple who are otherwise in conflict or at odds with each other. As such relationships may become rigid and routine as the couple try to keep their relationship intact but without wanting to face the many distressing aspects that have developed in their interactions together. Couples, resources allowing, will seek help from relationship or sex therapists to help them to refocus on their intimacy. The couple need to find ways of changing their tried and trusted yet dry and rigid communication styles. To do so means facing the pain and losses that have developed between them.

Lori Boul helps couples on this often long and difficult process of change by making the pathway more manageable. Lori's writing style and delivery of advice helps to maintain optimism by providing key educational points, practical exercises and by reintroducing fun and the unexpected into the relationship.

This book delivers the information that makes it unnecessary for individuals in unhappy relationships to have to search out their own therapist. The book provides an easy-to-read format, a warm and welcome invitation into the therapist's room, while all the time the couple are working at their own pace in their own homes.

Lori helps to relieve the frustration that many couples face who are in love but whose structures do not allow them to relate well with each other to find hope and to move forwards again. As an experienced therapist and clinician who has worked with many couples in distress, in both the independent sector and the National Health Service, to help them find new pathways and hope, Lori offers couples realistic expectations in straightforward language. The model of self-help for couple relationships and sexuality incorporates confronting the misunderstandings and myths that develop over time, and which may be life-long, in pursuit of healthy relationships and sexual growth.

Enjoy what you are about to read and, more importantly, enjoy putting the suggestions into practice.

Kevan Wylie MD, Consultant in Sexual Medicine, Sheffield, UK

Acknowledgements

I am indebted to Kevan Wylie, whose guidance and support have helped shape my work as a therapist. His development of integrated models of therapy, combining the most commonly used and reliable approaches to couples' problems in a logical framework, has been a source of inspiration for *DIY Sex & Relationship Therapy*.

To the reviewers of this book, a special word of thanks for their time and diligence in working through the exercises. Reviewers who read the drafts and provided valuable feedback include: Rachel and Shane Kelley, Kate and Phil Means, Leslie and Stuart Pearson, Debbie Dennant and Tracy Moore, Carol Daniels and Alex Green.

And I am grateful to all the clients with whom I have had the privilege of working. It is their questions, openness and hard work that have motivated me to write this book.

Pre-therapy

- Are you experiencing problems in your intimate relationship that you don't seem to be able to resolve?

- Do you feel your relationship has become stale over the years and needs reviving?

- Are you reluctant to seek help from a relationship therapist because of the costs and time involved, long waiting lists or embarrassment?

- Have you tried reading self-help books about relationships but found them to be of little practical use?

If you have answered 'Yes' to one or more of the above, then this book can help you. Whether you are female or male, no matter how long you have been with your partner or what kind of relationship you have, it will help you to overcome your problems. It will teach you skills that can make your intimate relationships more satisfying and assist you in rekindling the fun and romance.

Why DIY therapy?

You are the *real* experts in your relationship. During my work as a therapist, both in the NHS and private practice, I have helped many couples develop their relationship and sexual expertise. Yet, ultimately, their success has been of their own making. Fundamentally, most of this success is achieved by couples in their own homes through the use of homework exercises, designed to teach the skills necessary to make changes in their relationships.

While some people might question the effectiveness of self-help manuals, research has shown that it is possible to overcome problems without professional help. In *DIY Sex & Relationship Therapy*, you will find the information, techniques and practical homework exercises I use in face-to-face therapy to help couples overcome problems and enhance their relationships.

What is DIY therapy?

Broadly speaking, in sex and relationship therapy individuals and couples are provided with expert guidance, support and encouragement to help them understand and communicate their problems and to reinstate or improve their intimacy. Much of the work undertaken by the therapist is in providing information, acting as a facilitator or mediator in discussions and suggesting 'homework' exercises to be carried out between therapy sessions.

DIY therapy includes the techniques used with couples in face-to-face therapy. It is based on the therapeutic process, covering specific aspects of sex and relationship issues. Importantly, this book provides:

- practical guidance offered to couples in therapy sessions;

- homework exercises used by relationship therapists;

- additional techniques, which include DIY therapy cards that will help you to put the fun and romance back into your relationship.

How to use this book

The chapters in this book are referred to as 'sessions', since each one contains information and homework exercises used in face-to-face therapy. If you want to replicate the therapy process, you will need to work through each session in turn.

As you read through the book, you might want to look for sections that specifically address your difficulties. But before you start, I'd like to point out that one of the most important things at the beginning of therapy is to ensure that couples are able to talk to each other about their problems. So if you decide to start with a session that you believe is particularly important to you, first make sure you check out Session 1, 'Talking to each other', before you start your DIY therapy.

The following four icons have been used throughout this book to help organise the material and identify important points.

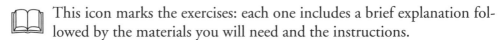 This icon marks the exercises: each one includes a brief explanation followed by the materials you will need and the instructions.

This icon highlights an important point or idea to remember.

☺ This icon indicates when you have work to do alone.

☯ When you see this icon, it means you will be working with your partner.

Throughout this book you will notice that I use the broad terms of partners and relationships instead of referring to wives, husbands and marriage. While I accept that for some people this might appear to be yet another irritating example of 'political correctness', it is in no way intended to denigrate the traditions of religious or civil bonds. My choice of these terms is simply a reflection of the diversity of individuals and couples I have worked with. Heterosexual and homosexual couples of all ages, people living apart, living together and in marital relationships have all successfully used the techniques included in this book.

Can I work through this book on my own?

Yes, it is possible to use this book on your own and gain some insight into your relationship. But, as in face to face couple therapy, you will gain most benefits by working with your partner.

How much time do we need on DIY therapy?

On average, most couples have between ten and 20 sessions with a therapist, each one lasting up to one hour. Between sessions, couples would be expected to undertake homework assignments, which could take another two to three hours a week.

DIY therapy follows a similar process to face-to-face therapy. Each of the sessions in this book consists of a week's typical therapy work (three to four hours), so you should expect to spend at least the same amount of time. In DIY therapy you have the advantage of being able to do the work at a time suitable to you. What is important is that you don't rush the steps within this process.

How can we know if we're making progress?

When you are putting a lot of time and effort into anything, it is important to be able to see your progress. During the first session in therapy couples are often asked to think about and write down what particular goals they would like to achieve. These goals are reviewed periodically to ensure they are on track and to change or add new goals that might have evolved from the work they have been doing.

At the end of this introduction you will find an exercise that will allow you to consider and prepare your own goals for your DIY therapy, which you will be able to review and update as you complete subsequent sessions.

From the Therapist's Chair

It takes a great deal of courage to admit you have a problem – and even more to make the changes necessary to resolve your issues. All the couples I work with start their therapy with some trepidation, wondering if it is going to work, or even work out the way they expect it to. My response is to tell them that therapy is a journey into the unknown; there are no guarantees that the changes they make will have the outcomes they expect. But if they don't make changes, the one thing that can be guaranteed is their relationship is more likely to stagnate or deteriorate than improve. The couples I have worked with have taken the risk of making changes; and the one quality that has ensured successful outcomes has been commitment. In self-help, as in therapy, both partners need to be willing to put in the time and effort needed towards finding a solution.

The following comments are from couples who have made the commitment and spent just a few hours a week using the techniques and tools included in this book.

> *To start with, I was terrified and embarrassed – but it was all worth it. We both understand each other on a deeper level and our relationship is enriched.*

> *We really enjoyed using the cards. The strangers' meeting was great fun. I never realised my partner was so inventive.*

> *Putting the romance back into our relationship helped us see our problems in a different light.*

Points to ponder

- You are the experts on your relationship, which means you can make it work.

- Making a commitment to spend just a few hours a week working on your relationship can restore and reinvigorate it.

- Agreeing your goals and monitoring your progress will keep you on track.

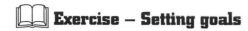 **Exercise – Setting goals**

Before starting your DIY therapy, you should think about the goals you would like to achieve. These goals will be different for every couple, and they also might differ for each partner. Do bear in mind that, as in other areas of life, the goals you set must be realistic and will demand some time and effort in order to achieve them.

Materials required

- Paper, two envelopes and pen or pencil

Instructions

☺ *Working alone*

1. Write down on a piece of paper **three** relationship goals that you would like to achieve, for example:

   - I'd like us to argue less;

   - I'd like the romance back in our lives;

   - I'd like our sex life to be more exciting.

2. When you have finished, **do not** discuss each other's goals.

3. Put your goals sheets in separate sealed envelopes, write your names on the envelopes and put them away somewhere safe until you have completed the exercises in 'Session 1, Talking to each other'.

As you work through the book, check back on your goals and acknowledge successes by rewarding each other.

- In therapy, couples sometimes exchange tokens (for example, coloured beads or marbles) as a visible reminder of the work they have done together and what they have achieved.

- If, as you progress, you develop new ideas about your relationship, you might want to change existing goals or add new ones.

Session 1
Talking to each other

When a couple first attends therapy, it is often difficult for them to discuss their issues. In fact, communication in the early sessions of therapy frequently mirrors what is happening at home. Both partners may talk but they don't really listen to each other. Their conversations are often full of accusations, which result in one or both trying to defend their own behaviour. Some people fear that if they mention even the smallest of issues their partner will get upset.

Since these communication difficulties can be the cause or result of a couple's problems, the first task of a therapist is to find ways to guide their conversations in directions that will help them identify the real issues. Initially the therapist acts as a mediator to ensure that couples listen and respond appropriately to each other.

At home, couples don't have the advantage of a 'referee' to help them overcome the defensive barriers they have erected. But as therapy progresses, the communication style the therapist employs works as a training model that couples can use outside therapy sessions. Having successfully worked with numerous couples, I know it is possible for them to act as their own mediators. By learning certain techniques, they are well equipped to discuss their issues without the help of a therapist.

In DIY therapy, as in face-to-face therapy, the first step is to be able to talk to each other in a safe and non-threatening way. This session starts with some examples and simple exercises I have used in face-to-face therapy sessions and as homework exercises. Working through each of the exercises is vital before you try to deal with the more difficult issues at the end of this session and those covered later in the book.

Talking AT or WITH

Before you start your discussions it is important to understand that couples who argue a lot tend to talk 'at' rather than 'with' each other. Lecturing, nagging, moaning and accusing your partner are talking 'at'. The partner on the receiving end can become defensive, aggressive, or even conveniently deaf and withdraw from further interaction. When couples find it difficult to discuss their problems and get frustrated or angry, the original issue soon becomes lost in unhealthy communication. Some couples may get to the point where they can hardly hold a proper discussion about anything that really matters. Yet, as difficult as it may seem, communication barriers can be conquered. I have worked with people who have spent years talking 'at' each other, but when they learned to talk 'with' their partners, they were able to identify and resolve their problems.

The following example illustrates a typical conversation where both partners are talking *at* each other and not listening.

Sam: We haven't had sex for nearly a year. Be honest, you're just not interested in sex any more, are you? Or is it me you're not interested in?

Sue: You're exaggerating; it's not that long. Besides, I am so busy with work and the children and I am tired when it gets to bedtime. So what do you expect?

In this discussion, Sam is accusing Sue of not being interested in sex, but Sue doesn't answer the accusation or respond to his question about not being interested in him. Instead, she defends herself with reasons for not having sex. Without the therapist's intervention, the conversation might stop there or develop into an argument.

If we look at the same conversation with the intervention of a therapist, we can see how the therapist ensures that what is being said is being heard and understood.

Therapist: Would you like to tell me what you think your main problem is?

Sam: Well, we haven't had sex for nearly a year and I don't think Sue is interested in sex any more.

Therapist: So it has been a long time since you have had sex and you don't think Sue is interested in sex. Is that correct?

Sam: Yes, that's about it.

Therapist: Sue, would you like to respond to what Sam has just said?

Sue: Well, I am so busy with the children and everything and I am tired when it gets to bedtime.

Therapist:	I have heard what you have just said about being busy and being tired and I would like to come back to that. But could you tell me if you are interested in having sex with Sam?
Sue:	Well, yes, I would like to have sex with him.

In this conversation, the female therapist listens to Sam, acknowledges her understanding by repeating what Sam says, and checks her understanding before asking Sue to respond. When Sue responds with a defensive statement, the therapist first acknowledges Sue's response but then asks her to respond to Sam's statement about not being interested in sex. With the therapist's help, Sue answers the question, which means that the conversation is more likely to continue without accusations, thereby making it more likely that the couple will find a solution.

Using the PACT technique

In the above conversation the therapist was using a basic communication technique that involves four steps, or stages, easily remembered by the acronym **PACT.**

- **P**ay attention to what is being said by looking at the person speaking. Show how you are listening with gestures such as nodding your head. And what's very important, don't interrupt.

- **A**cknowledge what has been said by restating it in your own words.

- **C**heck from your partner's response to see if what you said was accurate. If not, then amend what you said and restate.

- **T**hink before speaking and respond without making accusations, assumptions or judgemental statements.

If we now return to Sue and Sam's conversation without a therapist and apply **PACT,** it might look like this:

	Sam:	We haven't had sex for nearly a year and I don't think you're really interested in sex.
Pay attention	**Sue:**	(*Looks at Sam and shows she is listening*)
Acknowledge and restate	**Sue:**	I know we haven't had sex for a long time, but do you really think it is because I am not interested?

Check	**Sam:**	I don't know what else to think, but you don't seem to be interested.
Think and respond	**Sue:**	I am interested in sex. It's just that I have been so busy and I am tired when it gets to bedtime.

By using the **PACT** technique, Sue answered Sam's question and left the door open for more discussion.

This example shows how using the **PACT** technique can help you improve communication, without the help of a therapist. However, my years of experience have taught me that it is often difficult for couples, especially those who have spent many years arguing, to stick to these methods in their homework exercises. Therefore, in order to help couples use the **PACT** method, particularly when discussing difficult issues that have previously caused arguments, I also provide them with the following **traffic light cards**.

TRAFFIC LIGHT CARDS

On page 7 you will find six **traffic light cards**, two marked 'GO', two 'THINK' and two 'STOP'. Cut these out and divide them so that you and your partner both have one of each. When you are discussing the topics in the exercises in this session, or any of those in the subsequent sessions, use the cards in the following way.

The STOP card

Hold up this card if you want the conversation to STOP because the person talking:

- appears to be getting angry or is frightening you in any way;

- says something you find hurtful or is blaming you;

- is straying from the topic and/or referring to past events.

When the STOP card has been used:

1. Both you and your partner should stop talking immediately and remain silent for three minutes.

    - During this time you can go out of the room (for example, to make a cup of tea or walk round the garden).

When the three minutes have passed, hold up the GO card to indicate that you are ready to resume your conversation. Explain to your partner why you needed to hold up the STOP Card. Tell them about the way you felt (for example, afraid, hurt, angry, confused) – without accusations or blame.

The THINK card

Use this card if you want the conversation to pause to allow you time to think because:

- you don't understand what your partner is saying or what they mean;
- your partner has said a number of things that you are finding difficult to take in.

When the THINK card has been used:

1. The person talking should stop immediately.
2. The partner listening should explain briefly what they don't understand.
3. The person talking should try to find a better way to say what they mean.

The GO card

Hold up the GO card when:

- you are ready to resume a paused or stopped conversation;
- you like something your partner has said.

Important

 Use these **traffic light cards** throughout the following exercises in this book, until you *both* consider that they are no longer necessary.

📖 Exercise 1 – Neutral conversations

In this first exercise you will be talking about neutral topics that will help you practise your DIY therapy skills using the **PACT** technique and **traffic light cards**.

It is important that you remember to stick to the topic and a time limit for what you want to say. This will help you avoid straying off to sensitive or difficult discussions, and also ensure that your partner can summarise what you have said.

Materials required

- Traffic light cards

- Clock

Instructions

1. Choose one of the following topics:

    - a television programme or film you have watched;

    - a writer, film/sports star, singer or celebrity you like;

    - a holiday destination that you would like to visit;

    - a book, magazine or newspaper article you have read, or a news item you found interesting.

2. One partner should talk about the chosen topic for **two minutes only**.

    - This will help to ensure that your partner can summarise what you have said.

3. Follow the four **PACT** steps for each topic.

    - **P**ay attention to what is said by looking at the person who is speaking and really listening to them. Show how you are listening with gestures such as nodding your head. And – this is very important – don't interrupt.

    - **A**cknowledge what has been said by restating it in your own words.

    - **C**heck from your partner's response to see if what you said was accurate. If not, then amend what you said and restate.

    - **T**hink before speaking and respond without making accusations, assumptions or judgemental statements.

4. When you have completed the **PACT** steps, do not discuss the topic further; move on to the next topic.

5. When each of you has talked about **two** of the topics, and **both** are happy that you are following the **PACT** technique, you can move on to Exercise 2.

Don't forget to use your **traffic light cards** if you need time to think about what is being said.

TRAFFIC LIGHT CARDS

The STOP Card

Both you and your partner should stop talking immediately and remain silent for three minutes.

When the three minutes have passed, hold up the GO card to indicate you are ready to resume your conversation.

Explain to your partner why you needed to hold up the STOP card.

The STOP Card

Both you and your partner should stop talking immediately and remain silent for three minutes.

When the three minutes have passed, hold up the GO card to indicate you are ready to resume your conversation.

Explain to your partner why you needed to hold up the STOP card.

The THINK Card

The person talking should stop.

The partner listening should explain briefly what they didn't understand.

The person talking should try to find a better way to say what they mean.

The THINK Card

The person talking should stop.

The partner listening should explain briefly what they didn't understand.

The person talking should try to find a better way to say what they mean.

The GO Card

Hold up this card when:

you are ready to resume a paused or stopped conversation;

you like something your partner has said.

The GO Card

Hold up this card when:

you are ready to resume a paused or stopped conversation;

you like something your partner has said.

Exercise 2 – Talking about you

Now it's time to get a little more personal. In this exercise, you will be talking about personal issues that do not directly involve your partner. It is important to remember that it is not about what your partner might have done or said to you. Talk only about you and things you experienced. To make sure your discussion doesn't become one more episode in whatever unresolved conflicts you may have, follow the **PACT** method and stick to the topics provided.

Materials required

- Traffic light cards

- Clock

Instructions

🌐 *Working together*

1. Choose one of the following topics:

    - something good that happened to you today;

    - something that saddened you today;

    - something difficult you had to deal with today;

    - something that made you happy today.

2. One partner should talk about the chosen topic for **two minutes only**.

    - This will help to ensure that your partner can summarise what you have said.

3. Follow the four **PACT** steps for each topic.

    - **P**ay attention to what is said by looking at the person who is speaking and really listening to them. Show how you are listening with gestures such as nodding your head. And – this is very important – don't interrupt.

    - **A**cknowledge what has been said by restating it in your own words.

    - **C**heck from your partner's response to see if what you said was accurate. If not, then amend what you said and restate.

    - **T**hink before speaking and respond without making accusations, assumptions or judgemental statements.

4. When you have completed the **PACT** steps, do not discuss the topic further; move on to the next topic.

5. When each of you has talked about **two** of the topics, and **both** are happy that you are following the **PACT** technique, you can move on to Exercise 3.

Use your **Traffic light cards** if you need to.

Dealing with arguments

I should like to make it clear that arguments per se are not necessarily a problem. When we live with someone, we are bound to have differences of opinion at times. Some couples find an occasional heated discussion stimulating, invigorating, even sexually exciting – and enjoy the making up! This is quite different from couples in conflict, whose discussions can easily turn into bitter arguments, which are rarely resolved. If you and your partner are locked in conflict, you are unlikely to recognise or agree on what is causing the arguments.

Couples in conflict frequently complain about such things as lack of support with domestic chores or differences of opinion about childcare, money, sex or how they spend their free time. But I am aware that what they *say* the arguments are about is not necessarily the whole story.

Read the following fairly typical situation of Alice and Alan, and see if you can identify what their problems might be. Then turn to the end of this session for an answer.

> *Alice and Alan have been happily married for seven years but since the birth of their baby they have been arguing. Alice complains that Alan never helps with the baby or with housework. Alan disagrees and says that he does help. Their constant arguments usually result in their avoiding each other, often for days. Consequently, they have not been intimate with each other for over six months.*

Exercise 3 – Difficult discussions

Now it's time to get even more personal. I have provided you with some of the tools and techniques so that you can begin to discuss the issues that may be affecting your relationship. In this exercise you will be talking to your partner about something they have done in the past week that has upset you.

Before you start this exercise it is important to realise that you need to focus on how *you* feel and how your partner's actions affect you, rather than on his or her supposed failings. A good formula for expressing emotions is to use 'I' statements that let your partner know how you feel, rather than 'You' statements, which are more likely to make your partner feel hostile and defensive. For example, it is better to say something like '*I get upset when you come home late without letting me know, because I worry about you,*' than '*You never let me know when you are going to be late. You don't care about my feelings.*' The first statement gives your partner an opportunity to respond to your feelings whereas the second is more likely to trigger an argument.

Do keep in mind that the aim of this exercise is not to criticise or blame; it is about effectively communicating rather than solving any particular problems. In a one-hour session of therapy, there are usually several issues to be discussed, which cannot all be resolved within this time frame. Therefore, a time limit of ten minutes is recommended for talking about each problem.

Materials required

- Pen or pencil

- Clock

- Traffic light cards

Instructions

☺ *Working alone*

Write down one thing your partner has done in the past week that has upset you. It is very important to use **one** – and only one – very specific example like:

- I was hurt on Wednesday when you said I looked a mess because I worried you don't find me attractive any more.

- I was upset last night when you didn't want to have sex because I thought I had done something wrong.

- I was concerned by the amount of money you spent when we went out on Thursday because I am afraid we can't afford it.

- I was worried about you on Monday when you didn't telephone to let me know you would be late.

☯ *Working together*

1. Tell your partner about the specific issue that upset you, stick to the topic and allow a **10-minute time** limit for discussion.

2. Follow the **PACT** method.

- **P**ay attention to what is said by looking at the person who is speaking and really listening to them. Show how you are listening with gestures such as nodding your head. And – this is very important – don't interrupt.

- **A**cknowledge what has been said by restating it in your own words.

- **C**heck from your partner's response to see if what you said was accurate. If not, then amend what you said and restate.

- **T**hink before speaking and respond without making accusations, assumptions or judgemental statements.

3. When the **10 minutes** have passed, the other partner takes their turn to talk about their specific issue.

Use your **Traffic light cards** if you need to.

 This exercise is about practice in dealing with difficult discussions, as well as gaining some understanding about how our behaviour may cause conflict. Resolving conflicts requires reviewing and agreeing on your goals.

Exercise 4 – Agreeing your goals

You have worked through the discussion techniques. It is now time to review your individual goals and agree with your partner on your shared goals.

Materials

- Goals sheets envelopes

- Pen or pencil and sheet of paper

- Traffic light cards

Instructions

 Working together

1. Open the envelopes containing your goals sheets and discuss the three goals you each wrote.

2. Discuss and agree what you want to achieve or change in your relationship.

3. Write your agreed goals on one sheet of paper and put it in a prominent place so you can keep on track.

   - Be aware that you will probably have to compromise and your goals should be realistic.

4. As you work through the book, check back on your goals and change existing goals or add new ones.

Remember

 Your goals should be about what both of you want to achieve in your relationship and **not** about how you want your partner to change.

From the Therapist's Chair

 Good communication is the cornerstone of any relationship, sexual or otherwise. For this reason, improving communications is one of the first and main goals of therapy. Although most of the couples I work with are well educated and eloquent communicators, they are often unable to express themselves or understand their partners when it comes to discussing problems. It is perhaps not surprising that, when strong emotions are involved, if a message can be understood in more than one way, it will be understood in just the way that causes most harm.

Whatever the issue, improving communication can help prevent misunderstandings and resolve the resentments that so often cause and maintain problems. Indeed, many couples are surprised to find how quickly they can improve their relationships and overcome issues simply by learning some basic communication techniques.

The exercises in this session have been based on exercises and homework assignments I use at the start of therapy. If you continue to use the conversation techniques you have learned with the exercises in the following sessions, you will be well on the way to resolving your problems.

Points to ponder

- Talking 'at' is not the same as talking 'with' each other.

- Pay attention when your partner is talking.

- Think about the consequences of your responses and actions.

- Don't speak or act when you are angry.

- Communicating better doesn't mean you will no longer have any problems or that you will always agree. What it does mean is that you will be better equipped to deal with difficulties when they arise.

Case study

ALICE AND ALAN – THE REAL PROBLEM

On the surface, Alice and Alan's arguments appear to be about shared domestic work. While it is possible that Alan isn't pulling his weight, the fact that their arguments resulted in avoiding intimacy suggests there could be other issues. It is not unusual for couples to argue about seemingly trivial issues because they find it difficult to talk about deeper problems.

Therefore, Alice and Alan's problems could be that one or both of them:

- are having problems adapting to parenthood;

- have a sexual difficulty, which is often typified by avoidance strategies;

- feel neglected;

- are afraid of another pregnancy.

Session 2
Identifying the problems

When you have a medical problem, your GP asks you to describe the symptoms you are experiencing. From these symptoms, the doctor attempts to make a diagnosis and prescribe treatment. When couples seek help from a relationship therapist, the starting point is usually to ask them to describe the problems they are experiencing. But, unlike medical conditions, relationship problems aren't as simple to explain or categorise as infections, disease, broken limbs, or aches and pains.

Couples in conflict often find it difficult to identify or agree on what has caused their problem. Even when they do agree, they have different perceptions of the issues, which can make the solution harder to find. Sometimes the original cause can be long forgotten, yet the pain and recriminations remain.

Therapists can help couples explore the source of conflict by asking questions and offering alternative explanations. They can also act as a 'referee' to prevent discussions leading to more conflict. Ultimately, it is the couple themselves who work out what the problems are and how to resolve them. Using the conversation skills and techniques (**PACT** and **traffic light cards**) from the previous session will help you discuss your problems without a 'referee'. However, all the talking in the world (on your own or with a therapist) will not resolve a problem. You need to decide on the actions required to change a situation and then carry them out. It is important that you try to find a mutually agreeable plan of action that will lead to a solution.

This session includes some of the most common issues couples bring to therapy, together with exercises to help you identify and resolve your particular issues. As in face-to-face therapy I start with a 'therapy contract', which is used to ensure that couples are in agreement about the way they will work together.

Remember

When you have worked through the exercises in this chapter, review your relationship goals.

DIY therapy contract

At the start of therapy, most therapists ask couples to agree how they will work together to resolve their problems and to write their own set of 'rules' into a contract. These 'therapy contracts' are used to ensure that clients understand what is and is not acceptable in therapy sessions, and to guide their discussions throughout the course of their therapy.

Detailed below is a contract containing a minimum set of rules I would expect couples to follow in therapy sessions. Before you begin to discuss your issues, it is important that you both agree on these rules (adding any of your own) and show your agreement to abide by them by signing your contract.

Our Contract

1. I have a right to my own opinions and beliefs.

2. I will respect your opinions and beliefs and will not patronise or dismiss them just because they don't match mine.

3. I have the right to say no.

4. I will respect your right to say no.

5. I will not try to cajole, bully or manipulate you into agreeing with what I want.

6. I will not rake up the past.

7. I will carry out agreed actions, within agreed timescales.

8. I agree to try to be open and honest in all our discussions.

9. I agree to give you the opportunity to express your fears and worries without recrimination.

10. I will not be verbally or physically aggressive towards you.

Declaration

We declare that we will try to keep each other's best interests at the forefront of our thoughts, words and actions at all times.

Name .... Signed ....

Name .... Signed ....

In face-to-face therapy, I have found that people who agree to make changes just to please or placate their partner are rarely able to keep their promises. In a relationship, things can only change if both partners freely and willingly agree to make the changes.

Exercise 1 – Identifying problems

At the end of this session you will find two copies of the 'Identifying Problems' questionnaire, which contains 30 statements (typically made by couples in therapy) under the following six topic headings:

- Affection

- Appreciation

- Family and friends

- Money

- Time

- Trust

By completing the questionnaire you can identify specific issues and then turn to the heading for that topic in this session to find a brief explanation and exercise instructions.

Materials required

- 'Identifying Problems' questionnaire

- Pen or pencil

Instructions

 ☺ *Working alone*

Using the 'Identifying Problems' questionnaire, tick the boxes that you feel correspond to your viewpoints.

- This is not a competition – it is not about how well you score. This questionnaire is simply a means to help you identify the topics you wish to address.

Working together

1. Compare your answers to the questions with your partner's and identify the topic where:

    *   your answers are different (for example, one of you has ticked 'Always true' and the other 'Never true' or 'Sometimes true').

    *   **Important**: Do not discuss these issues at this point.

2. Turn to the page containing the topic that you have identified as problematic and read the brief description.

    *   If you have identified more than one topic, it is important that you deal with only one at a time.

3. When you have both read the description of the problematic area(s) and had time to think about how you feel, follow the instructions for that topic exercise.

Remember

> **Do not discuss your issues until after you have scored the questionnaire and have referred to the instructions for that particular area.**

A word about sex

Sexual problems rarely start (or end) in the bedroom. It is rare to find couples who have sexual difficulties without relationship conflicts or vice versa. Unfortunately, it can be difficult to determine if sexual problems are causing a relationship difficulty or if relationship issues are causing sexual problems.

For this reason, in face-to-face therapy couples with sexual problems are asked to refrain from sex and from talking about sexual issues until they have a clearer understanding of their real issues. I would recommend that, in your DIY therapy, you follow the same process. This means refraining from sexual activities and from talking about sexual problems until you have both worked through the first five sessions of the book. Heeding this advice will ensure you have dealt with any relationship difficulties that could be affecting your love life.

Important

If the mind is willing but the body won't work, and you are sure you have no relationship problems, you might want to turn to Session 6, 'Let's talk about sex'. However, I would highly recommend that you come back to Session 5, 'Romance', since this session can help make a good thing even better.

Lacking affection

Many couples attending therapy complain that their partners aren't as affectionate as they used to be. A lack of affection can often make partners feel unloved, rejected or hurt. In order to protect their feelings, couples often create distance regulators, such as: *'You don't give me any affection so I am going to ignore you'*, or even: *'You are ignoring me so I am going to get affection from someone else'*. Unfortunately, over time, the distance between couples can become so great that it is difficult for either partner to ask for affection or make the first move.

In therapy I usually ask couples to start with something small that they can do for each other. For example, couples who haven't been affectionate for years often sit on separate chairs (or even in separate rooms), so they might agree to sit on the sofa together when they are watching television. Another starting point could be that they agree to greet each other every evening with a kiss, or simply hold hands when out walking.

The affection exercise overleaf is designed to help you to rekindle the warmth and intimacy that may have been lost. Don't forget to continue with the **PACT** techniques and use the **traffic light cards** when needed, to help you avoid conflict.

It is **very important** that each partner is willing to make the first move without waiting for the other to show signs of encouragement. After all, it is not like a first meeting when you are unsure if the person you are approaching will be interested.

Exercise 2 – Affection

Materials required

- Paper and pen or pencil

- Traffic light cards

Instructions

☺ *Working alone*

- List five ways you would like your partner to show their affection for you.

- **Important**: in this exercise 'affection' does not mean 'sex'.

☯ *Working together*

1. Exchange lists and discuss the things you have both written.

2. Agree the things that you both feel comfortable doing.

3. Discuss the things you don't want or like to do and explain why.

4. Do one of the things from your partner's list now.

5. Put your lists in a prominent place to remind you to maintain your agreed actions.

Feeling unappreciated

Couples attending relationship therapy frequently complain that their partners don't appreciate them or that they take them for granted. What they usually mean is they feel neglected and unimportant.

It's a big mistake to assume that our partners know how important they are to us. They need to be told or shown how beautiful we think they are, how grateful we are for what they do and how much we appreciate their qualities. Both men and women need reassuring words and actions, especially in intimate relationships.

The problem of lack of appreciation often arises when people engage in something referred to in therapy as 'mind reading'. When we live with someone for any length of time, there is a tendency to assume that our partners know and understand us and there is no need to express our appreciation. Also, with the pace of modern living, it can become all too easy to forget to say or do the things that make our partner feel special.

The appreciation exercise below can help you understand what you both need to do to overcome the 'mind reading' trap and show your appreciation for each other.

Exercise 3 – Appreciation

Materials required

- Paper and pen or pencil

- Traffic light cards

Instructions

☺ *Working alone*

List five things you would like to hear your partner say about you. Begin your sentences with:

- I like …

- I appreciate …

- I value …

- I enjoy …

- I think you are a good/creative/helpful/supportive …

☯ *Working together*

1. Exchange lists and discuss the things you have both written.

2. Agree the things that you both feel comfortable saying.

3. Say one of the things from your partner's list **now**.

4. Put your lists in a prominent place to remind you to maintain your agreed actions.

Family and friends

Although family and friends can provide a valuable support network, particularly in times of difficulty, they can also create problems. It can be difficult to remain loyal to your partner and put their interests first when your children, family or friends are intruding or interfering in your relationship.

From my experience, conflict over relationships with family members and friends is often due to a lack of understanding or an inability to know how to deal with the 'intruder'. The following case study of a couple I worked with illustrates just such a problem and how it was resolved.

Claire and Charles had been married for two years when they came to see me. Throughout their marriage, Mary (who was Charles's mother) had been a constant presence in their relationship. She would telephone Charles once or twice a day and 'pop in' to see them without notice, sometimes bringing meals. She was continually instructing Claire on how to do the housework and would even try to take over when she visited. Claire had complained to her husband about his mother on numerous occasions, but all Charles could see was his mother as he had always seen her – supportive and helpful.

While exploring this issue in therapy, Claire complained, 'Mary is always interfering. Nothing I do is ever good enough for her – she doesn't think I am a good wife.' But Charles heard this as: 'I don't like your mother and, since you are not able to control her, you are not much of a man.' This might all sound a bit irrational, but when family loyalties and strong emotions are concerned, we are rarely rational.

After Claire and Charles had discussed the issues further, Claire recognised that Mary was not necessarily criticising either her or her skills, but was probably lonely. When Charles realised that Claire was not criticising his masculinity, nor did she dislike his mother, he accepted that his mother's behaviour was upsetting Claire and interfering with their relationship. As a result, Charles decided to ask his mother not to phone so often and to visit only on specific days at prearranged times.

Resolving these types of situation isn't easy. What is sometimes perceived as interference by family or friends can be explained in other terms such as misguided concern, loneliness or a need to feel useful, needed and wanted. Recognising these issues can help you deal with the problem and stay united without alienating family and/or friends.

> **Important**
>
> A problem for one partner is a problem for both. A family member or friend might not be causing a problem for you, but if your partner is finding their behaviour or actions difficult, it is vital to address the issue.

Exercise 4 – Family and friends

Materials required

- Paper and pen or pencil

- Traffic light cards

Instructions

 ### ☺ *Working alone*

Write the name of the person you believe is interfering in your relationship and what it is they are doing that upsets you – try to be specific.

☯ *Working together*

1. Tell your partner what you believe the problem is and why you think it might be happening.

2. Discuss the issue (remember to use the **PACT** model and **traffic light cards**).

3. Do not use accusatory statements; tell your partner how the situation is making you feel.

4. Agree your solution and **stand united**.

Important

> If you have agreed to talk to the person who is causing the problem, it is vital that **you** tell your own family member or friend, preferably in the presence of your partner. This can prevent future misunderstandings and ensure that you show a united front.

Money conflicts

Although it is often said that money doesn't bring happiness, it can certainly create conflicts. Financial difficulties are bound to create a strain on any relationship, but conflicts over money – how it's earned, spent and saved – are more often about control and power than about actual financial difficulties.

Control and power conflicts can be both complex and explosive. People often believe that the partner who makes the decisions causes the problems. But control and power can also be wielded in a passive way. Partners who don't accept responsibility can be just as controlling as those who seem to hold the reins. Issues of power and control are covered in some detail in Session 3, 'Relationship Behaviours'. Meanwhile, I often start by encouraging couples to discuss money for what it is – a commodity that should support your relationship. It is not a commodity that defines who you are or a means to control your partner.

When actual financial concerns are causing conflict, the solution is in sharing responsibility. Resolving money problems can be quite straightforward. You should both know what's happening to your money and what you can or cannot afford. Importantly, you should be able to talk openly without fear of blame.

The money matters exercise below has been designed to help you to discuss issues about actual money concerns, as well as your feelings about them.

Exercise 5 – Money matters

Materials required

- Paper and pen or pencil

- Traffic light cards

Instructions

☯ *Working together*

1. Agree a specified time, when you are calm and not tired or angry, to discuss your financial situation.

   - If either of you is unsure of your financial situation, make a list of **all** your income and outgoings.

2. Discuss your finances but do not make demands. Instead, ask questions such as the following.

   - Can we agree on how much money each of us has for our own expenses?

   - How can we resolve our present financial difficulties?

   - What additional efforts could we make?

   - Should we seek professional advice?

3. Agree a course of action that you can both achieve.

4. Write down your agreed actions and put them in a prominent place as a reminder.

Being short of quality time together

Time is the most precious and important thing you can give to your part-ner. But issues of time are a problem in many relationships. Work and family commitments can seem to make it almost impossible for couples to have enough time alone together. Without realising it, partners can soon become housemates – strangers sharing the same accommodation.

Calculating how much time we spend together and what we do with it isn't always easy, particularly since partners might not always agree. In a week, there are 168 hours. If we take off the time we spend at work (say 40 hours) and sleeping (say 56 hours), we are left with the time we spend doing every-thing else (in this case 72 hours). The time exercise below will help you work out how much time you spend on various activities in a week so that you can ensure you have some quality time together.

It is **important** to remember that in an intimate relationship it isn't just about the amount of time you spend together, but the **quality** of your time together. For example, couples in long-distance relationships might only spend one weekend a month together, but in that weekend their time is completely devoted to each other.

 Exercise 6 – Time

Materials required

- Time worksheets (you will find these at the end of this session)

- Paper and pen or pencil

- Traffic light cards

Instructions

☺ *Working alone*

Using the time worksheet, allocate the amount of time you spend on each of the items listed (your total hours in one week are 168).

☯ *Working together*

1. Swap worksheets and discuss your responses.

2. If you have allocated little or no time in items 8 to 12, agree how much time you both want and **can** realistically reallocate from items 1 to 7. It doesn't matter if it's all your waking hours or just an hour a week – as long as you agree.

3. Write down your agreed actions, the time and activities you will share, and put them in a prominent place as a reminder.

Losing trust

One of the key components of any relationship is trust: it improves communication, promotes commitment and provides security. Of course, loving and trusting another person is risky because they might die, leave, wound, reject us or be unfaithful. But it's a risk we have to take if we want a loving relationship.

In many relationships, sexual infidelity is often the primary reason for loss of trust. I have worked with many couples when one, or both, partners have been unfaithful. When a partner has been unfaithful, people invariably ask: '*Why have they done this to me?*' My answer is always: '*They haven't done it to you: they have done it because they wanted to.*'

This might sound harsh. Yet the reality is that no one can make you be unfaithful unless you want to be.

Many people believe that the first step to regaining trust is admitting being at fault. You might be surprised to hear that I do not agree with this sentiment. Couples inevitably have differing opinions on where the bigger portion of blame lies and who is responsible for restoring the trust. It is often supposed that the partner who is perceived to be 'at fault' should show understanding for the feelings of the partner who has been 'hurt'. This kind of supposition usually results in the 'at fault' partner constantly trying to placate the 'hurt' partner. However, the feelings of the 'at fault' partner are rarely acknowledged or addressed.

In order to heal the relationship, couples must accept that in some way both partners contributed to the situation and both need understanding. In a relationship, both partners contribute (to some degree) to the problems they experience.

Ultimately, it doesn't matter how the trust has evaporated. If you are going to stay with your partner, you have to work together to re-establish the trust. I have found that it is often the couple's discussions about fault – usually full of blame and recrimination – that cause the biggest problems. No amount of talking is likely to solve problems of lack of trust. If you are determined to stay together, both of you will need to let go of blame and let your actions speak louder than words. For trust to be rebuilt and intimacy re-established, you must let go of the past and change your behaviour.

When promises have been broken, trusting someone, or proving you are trustworthy, isn't easy. Doing the following exercises doesn't mean you will forget: memories linger and recriminations can resurface. It won't be easy to overcome these painful memories, but it is necessary if you want to continue to cohabit without conflict and stop your past interfering with your future happiness.

Important

! Imagination and suspicions are usually worse than reality. While the truth might be difficult to hear, unfounded jealousy is far more toxic. Don't let your imagination rule your relationship – talk to your partner. If unfounded jealousy or self-esteem issues consume one partner, they might need further help from a therapist.

Exercise 7 – Trust: Despatching the past

It would be trite to suggest that couples can 'forgive and forget', since forgetting is impossible and forgiveness takes more than mere words. In this exercise you will be showing each other you are willing to try to re-establish trust by sharing in a symbolic activity.

Important

Before you begin this exercise, it is important to acknowledge that you are doing it not simply to please your partner but to free yourself from the influence of negative memories and feelings in order to move on.

Materials required

- Paper and pen or pencil

Instructions

☺ *Working alone*

Write down your own negative memories and feelings from your relationship.

- Do not discuss these with your partner.

☯ *Working together*

Take the pages and despatch them by doing something that is meaningful to you both. The following are some examples.

- Make a boat and set it adrift in the lake/river.

- Make an aeroplane and fly it from a hilltop.

- Tie it in a knot and burn it.

- Tear it up into small pieces and flush it down the toilet.

- Use it for bedding in your pet rabbit/hamster/gerbil's cage.

Exercise 8 – Trust: Promises

In order to establish or regain trust, it is important to make promises you can keep and keep the promises you make. Building trust is about establishing that you are reliable. It doesn't matter how small the promise is: if you make and keep promises every day, your partner will learn that you are reliable and can be trusted.

☺ *Working alone*

Write down some promises you can make and give them to your partner. The promises you make should be things that **you** are going to do – not what you want your partner to do. They could include some of the following statements.

- I will discuss my feelings if I am unhappy.

- I will not abuse you with recriminations about our past or threats for our future.

- I will be more attentive to your needs and desires.

- When I promise to be somewhere at a certain time I will be there.

- When I promise to do something I will do it.

☯ *Working together*

1. Give your partner your promises.

2. Write both sets of promises on one list and put it in a prominent place.

3. Rebuilding trust is a long and gradual process. Give each other time to prove you can trust and be trusted.

From the Therapist's Chair

In therapy, couples often start by blaming each other for past or imagined transgressions. While looking for the cause of conflict can help resolve a problem, blame usually results in feelings of disappointment or resentment, which can lead to frustration and anger. For this reason, whatever the problem may be and whoever started it, the couple must be committed to dealing with issues without blame or recriminations.

The problems presented in this session are typical of conflicts presented by couples in therapy, and should serve as a model for dealing with other issues. The exercises, together with the communication skills and techniques from Session 1, 'Talking to each other', should have helped you consider and deal with your own issues.

At this stage in your DIY therapy, I hope you have discovered that, providing you find time for each other and are learning to talk to each other in a constructive way, you don't need to spend an hour a week with a therapist.

Points to ponder

- Being happy in your relationship does not come automatically; it needs work.

- Resolving a relationship problem depends more on how you deal with conflict than the problem itself.

- Overcoming problems often means letting go of the past and putting an end to blame and recriminations.

- Showing your affection and appreciation are vital ingredients in a healthy relationship.

- The quality of the time you spend together is more important than the quantity.

IDENTIFYING PROBLEMS QUESTIONNAIRE

Name: _____

		Never true	Sometimes true	Always true
	Affection			
1	I like the way my partner shows her/his affection.			
2	My partner gives me lots of affection.			
3	My partner can be affectionate without it leading to sex.			
4	My partner is sensitive and aware of my needs.			
5	There is lots of warmth and affection in our relationship.			
	Appreciation			
6	My partner always thanks me when I do something for him/her.			
7	My partner regularly pays me compliments.			
8	My partner supports my beliefs and values.			
9	My partner encourages me in whatever I do.			
10	My partner is aware of how hard I work (in my job/at home etc.).			
	Family and friends			
11	My partner spends too much time with his/her parents (family).			
12	My partner's parents (family) interfere in our relationship.			
13	My partner's friends are a threat to our relationship.			
14	My partner puts his family before me.			
15	My partner puts his/her friends before me.			
	Money			
16	My partner and I always talk about our finances.			
17	My partner spends more money on him/herself than on me.			
18	We always make joint decisions on how money is spent or saved.			
19	I worry about our money problems			
20	I worry about my partner getting us into debt.			
	Time			
21	My partner and I have quality time alone together every day.			
22	My partner and I have quality time alone together every week.			
23	I try to spend as much time with my partner as I can.			
24	I feel neglected when my partner spends time on his/her own.			
25	I am happy with the amount of time my partner and I spend with others.			
	Trust			
26	I worry that my partner will be unfaithful.			
27	I worry that my partner might leave me.			
28	My partner is able to emotionally support me in difficult times.			
29	I find it easy to talk to my partner about my innermost feelings.			
30	I trust my partner to tell me when he/she has a problem.			

IDENTIFYING PROBLEMS QUESTIONNAIRE

Name: _____

		Never true	Sometimes true	Always true
	Affection			
1	I like the way my partner shows her/his affection.			
2	My partner gives me lots of affection.			
3	My partner can be affectionate without it leading to sex.			
4	My partner is sensitive and aware of my needs.			
5	There is lots of warmth and affection in our relationship.			
	Appreciation			
6	My partner always thanks me when I do something for him/her.			
7	My partner regularly pays me compliments.			
8	My partner supports my beliefs and values.			
9	My partner encourages me in whatever I do.			
10	My partner is aware of how hard I work (in my job/at home etc.).			
	Family and friends			
11	My partner spends too much time with his/her parents (family).			
12	My partner's parents (family) interfere in our relationship.			
13	My partner's friends are a threat to our relationship.			
14	My partner puts his family before me.			
15	My partner puts his/her friends before me.			
	Money			
16	My partner and I always talk about our finances.			
17	My partner spends more money on him/herself than on me.			
18	We always make joint decisions on how money is spent or saved.			
19	I worry about our money problems.			
20	I worry about my partner getting us into debt.			
	Time			
21	My partner and I have quality time alone together every day.			
22	My partner and I have quality time alone together every week.			
23	I try to spend as much time with my partner as I can.			
24	I feel neglected when my partner spends time on his/her own.			
25	I am happy with the amount of time my partner and I spend with others.			
	Trust			
26	I worry that my partner will be unfaithful.			
27	I worry that my partner might leave me.			
28	My partner is able to emotionally support me in difficult times.			
29	I find it easy to talk to my partner about my innermost feelings.			
30	I trust my partner to tell me when he/she has a problem.			

✂ ....

TIME WORKSHEET	Time
Name: _____	
1 Domestic chores (housework, cooking, gardening, DIY, childcare etc.)	
2 Visiting family	
3 Socialising with friends and colleagues etc.	
4 Watching the television	
5 Leisure time on the computer alone	
6 Hobbies alone	
7 Other solo activities	
8 Hobbies together	
9 Time alone talking with your partner (without distractions)	
10 Intimate activities with your partner (cuddling, kissing etc.)	
11 Sex	
12 Other joint activities	
SLEEP	
WORK	
TOTAL	168

✂ ....

TIME WORKSHEET	Time
Name: _____	
1 Domestic chores (housework, cooking, gardening, DIY, childcare etc.)	
2 Visiting family	
3 Socialising with friends and colleagues etc.	
4 Watching the television	
5 Leisure time on the computer alone	
6 Hobbies alone	
7 Other solo activities	
8 Hobbies together	
9 Time alone talking with your partner (without distractions)	
10 Intimate activities with your partner (cuddling, kissing etc.)	
11 Sex	
12 Other joint activities	
SLEEP	
WORK	
TOTAL	168

Session 3
Relationship behaviours

As you have discovered from Sessions 1 and 2, much of the initial work in relationship therapy focuses on reducing or eliminating conflict by allocating time to improving communication. But poor communication is not the only obstacle to a good relationship.

Each partner brings different strengths, opinions, expectations and beliefs to a relationship. In a healthy relationship these differences can provide spice or stimulation. In a troubled relationship, however, differences can create power struggles that may result in resentment.

This session begins with a 'reality check' on some of the myths and romantic notions that can distort expectations and influence relationship behaviours; the remainder of the session focuses on the dynamics of relationships. When therapists talk of dynamics in a relationship, they are referring to the way that couples interact with each other. As relationships develop, patterns of giving and receiving evolve into the unspoken rules that affect the bonds between people. The exercises in this session will help you identify these dynamics and replace unhelpful interactions with behaviours that can maintain and improve your relationship.

Relationship expectations and myths

We tend to enter into relationships swept up by passion and romance, with idealistic notions of what it is going to be like. Not surprising, perhaps, if we consider that many of our beliefs are based on romantic ideals which continue to be promoted by popular culture. Lamentably, such ideals can produce a dangerous mix of relationship truths, half-truths and fantasy, all of which influence our expectations.

RELATIONSHIP EXPECTATIONS

The expectation that relationships simply take care of themselves is a common, yet erroneous, notion. In the real world, they need to be main- tained, serviced and sometimes repaired or overhauled – rather like a car that is to remain roadworthy. Another common expectation is the idea of 'fusion', which leads us to believe that we should always be in total harmony and accord with our partners.

Contrary to some of the common relationship expectations, consider the following statements.

- Relationships are *not* natural or effortless. A successful relationship is dependent on the level of care, work and commitment that two people are prepared to put into it.

- Two individuals should *not* strive or expect to exist as one – our differences make us interesting.

- A breakdown in a relationship doesn't have to lead to a break-up – overcoming difficulties can make a relationship stronger.

Couples in therapy sometimes make emotional statements that reflect their unrealistic expectations. Since many of these can be damaging, it is important that you recognise and question the ideas you might hold about relationships. I have listed below some common relationship myths that can cause problems. As you read through them and their 'reality checks', think about any other ideas and expectations you might have that could be affecting your relationship.

RELATIONSHIP MYTHS

Myth: Couples must have common interests to bond them together.

Reality check: In a healthy relationship couples usually share some common values, which are more important than common interests. Different interests allow you to retain your individuality and add variety and spice to your relationship.

Myth: My partner should be perfect.

Reality check: Perfection (if it exists) is extremely rare on the human quality scale. You should make a point of celebrating what you most admire and respect about your partner.

Myth: If you're in love, you won't find other people attractive.

Reality check: Being in love doesn't mean you are blind to beauty. You can look all you like, as long as you don't make your partner feel inadequate.

Myth: Love is unconditional.

Reality check: Unconditional love might exist between parent and child, but in adult loving relationships there are conditions relating to qualities such as loyalty, commitment and reliability.

Myth:	My partner should make me happy.
Reality check:	No one can make you happy unless you are already open and receptive. You – and only you – are responsible for your own happiness.
Myth:	My partner should know how I feel without me having to tell them.
Reality check:	'Mind reading' probably causes more problems in relationships than anything else. Partners cannot read each other's minds, regardless of how well they think they know each other. No one can know how you feel unless you tell them.
Myth:	Our relationship would be good if my partner changed.
Reality check:	A partner is *not* a project. The only person you can change is yourself. If you want your partner to change, perhaps you should ask yourself why you chose them in the first place.
Myth:	Other people are happier than we are.
Reality check:	All you know about other people's relationships is what you see on the surface and what they tell you.
Myth:	Couples in good relationships never argue.
Reality check:	There will always be things you disagree about when you live with someone. It is not *if* you argue but *how* you argue that counts. Learn to agree to disagree and make compromises.
Myth:	When two people are in love, the sex should automatically be good.
Reality check:	Good sex is about knowing what both of you want, need and like. Unless you are able to talk to your partner, being in love will not guarantee good sex.

Relationship dynamics

The dynamics of relationships – how we behave and interact with our partners – depend on not only our beliefs and expectations, but also our experiences. Failure to understand the dynamics underlying relationships often makes it more difficult for people to resolve conflict and move beyond their current problems.

Most of the couples I work with are surprised when they realise that many of their unhelpful relationship behaviours have been (consciously or unconsciously) learned in childhood. As children, we learn how to cooperate, compete and control. Sometimes, we might use positive behaviours such as smiling, sharing and being affectionate. But there may be times when negative behaviours such as sulking, manipulating or bullying have helped us achieve what we want.

Our very early experiences may teach us which behaviours are successful with our parents. However, they may not necessarily be the best ones to carry on into adulthood. Take sulking as an example. Within an adult relationship, sulking may get us attention, but the attention we get might not satisfy our needs and can alienate our partners. Yet, people often continue to repeat such patterns of behaviour, which can create power issues and result in competition and confrontation.

Fortunately, despite our early learning experiences, we are capable of changing old habits and unhelpful behaviours into ones that can strengthen and enhance our relationship. We cannot change our childhood, which is in the past. But if we are aware of how our history has affected us, we can control what we do today.

Overcoming old habits

In order to help couples in therapy understand and change the dynamics of their relationships, I use a simplified version of Eric Berne's description of relationship behaviours. In brief, Berne suggested that within each person there is a capacity to act in three main ways, each of which may be dependent on the situation. The first behaviour is that of the Parent in us, who can be nurturing and caring (or controlling and critical). The second occurs when we assume the role of an Adult and will act logically and responsibly. The third occurs when we assume the role of the Child, who can accept support and play (or rebel and manipulate).

The following explanations and diagrams show some couple interactions using the Parent–Adult–Child descriptions in healthy and troubled relationships. These are followed by exercises that will enable you to identify your relationship dynamics and change unhelpful styles of behaviour.

POSITIVE BEHAVIOURS

In healthy relationships, the dynamics are positive, supportive and helpful. The balance in the relationship is equitable, meeting both partners' needs. Positive behaviours would include those shown opposite.

Parent	*Provides support and encouragement; is considerate about their partner's weaknesses and emphasises their strong points.*
Adult	*Works with their partner in making decisions; shows respect and is able to discuss matters logically.*
Child	*Accepts support from their partner; is able to play, have fun and enjoy sex with their partner.*

Healthy interactions – adult roles

The diagram below illustrates the two-way Adult–Adult interactions that are found in healthy relationships.

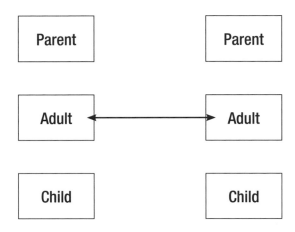

When going about normal day-to-day activities like dealing with family finances, domestic chores, childcare, etc., couples usually respond to each other in Adult–Adult mode by showing respect, discussing issues and working together to make decisions. The dynamics are positive, supportive and helpful and the balance in the relationship is equitable, meeting both partners' needs.

Healthy interactions – child roles

In the following diagram we have the two-way Child–Child interactions of a healthy relationship.

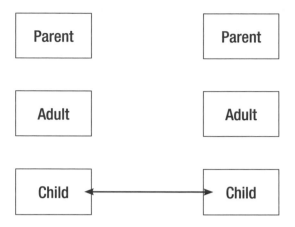

When couples are enjoying leisure time or more intimate moments, they both assume the Child–Child roles of playfulness and fun. One of the cornerstones of a healthy relationship is the amount of time couples 'play' together. Play is necessary, not only for our own relaxation and to relieve the stress of day-to-day living, but also because it can strengthen bonds and develop the creativity that can keep relationships alive.

Healthy parent–child interactions

The diagram below shows the two-way Parent–Child interactions of a healthy relationship.

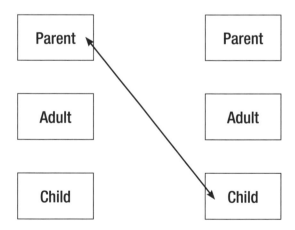

In certain situations, one role can *temporarily* become dominant; for example, when one partner is ill or upset and the other adopts a parental, nurturing role. The sick partner will respond by accepting the role of a cared-for child until they are well.

NEGATIVE BEHAVIOURS

In contrast, in troubled relationships, couples may often exhibit negative Parent or Child behaviours. When negative interactions are involved, the balance of power can become one-sided and dictated by one partner's needs. The diagram below shows a relationship in which one person attempts to treat their partner as an adult while the other is behaving like a controlling parent or manipulative child.

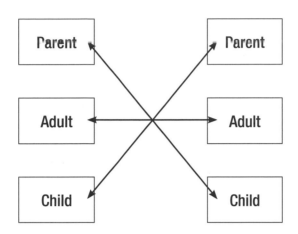

Adult   *attempts to share responsibility and discuss issue rationally.*
Child   *rebels or sulks to manipulate or to avoid responsibility.*
Parent   *controls, dominates and threatens, often through bullying or nagging.*

Negative Parent and/or Child behaviours are common types of control behaviours but they can backfire. A person who behaves like a negative Parent, by trying to control or dominate, is likely to force their partner into a negative Child role. Similarly, a person who behaves like a dependent or needy Child should not be surprised if their partner becomes a nagging Parent.

Unlike positive Parent–Child behaviours, temporarily adopted in times of need, negative Parent–Child relationships tend to be more enduring and often result in power struggles. If negative behaviours are not addressed, they can foster resentment, which is disastrous to any relationship. The following example of a couple I have worked with shows how people can fall into the trap of a habitual negative Parent–Child interaction.

David and Debbie, who had been together for six years, came to see me complaining that they hadn't had sex for nearly two years. It appeared that Debbie made all the financial decisions in their relationship, which suited them fine at the beginning. However, over time, Debbie found that she was making most of the decisions, not only financial, but also in decisions to do with the home and their social life. The more David avoided his responsibilities, the more Debbie felt that if she didn't take responsibility nothing would get done. Eventually, David became resentful and withdrew from Debbie and his responsibilities.

This extract illustrates the negative Parent–Child interactions between Debbie and David. Without realising it, the couple had developed a Controlling Parent–Resentful Child relationship. Their Adult–Adult interaction of shared decision-making was virtually non-existent, while their Child–Child interactions of play, fun and sex completely disappeared (not surprisingly, since David's behaviour led Debbie to see him as a dependent child). Debbie and David had failed to discuss what they needed from each other. They had settled into roles that were destroying their relationship. When they realised what was happening, they began to learn to relate to each other more as adults. As a result, they were able to have fun together and their sexual activity returned.

Remember

 If you keep on doing what you have been doing, you will keep on getting what you have been getting.

Exercise 1 – Relationship dynamics

This first exercise has been designed for you to consider what behaviours contribute to unhealthy relationship dynamics. You are provided with two examples of negative interactions, which are followed by negative statements for you to classify.

Materials required

- Paper and pen

Instructions

 Working together

Read the following examples of two communications, which show how healthy and unhealthy responses can occur in the most mundane situations. Note how they have been classified as Parent, Adult and Child interactions.

Example 1: Negative Child

Question: 'Did you take out the rubbish bins?'

Healthy response: 'No, dear – don't worry. I'll take them out before we go to bed.'
                        (**Adult → Adult**)

Unhealthy response: 'Will you stop nagging me.' (**Negative Child → Parent**)

Example 2: Negative Parent

Question.   'Did you take out the rubbish bins?'

Healthy response: 'No, dear – don't worry. I'll take them out before we go to bed.'
                        (**Adult → Adult**)

Unhealthy response: 'You should know by now that we can't take them out too early.'
                        (**Negative Parent → Child**)

Identifying roles

Read the following statements and put a tick in the corresponding box to indicate whether each statement might be made by a person behaving like a **negative** Parent or Child. (You'll find the answers at the end of this session.)

No.	Statement	Parent	Child
1	Don't be such a misery.		
2	You never do anything right.		
3	It's all in your mind – you're imagining it.		
4	You're no fun any more.		
5	You don't care about my feelings.		
6	You never tell me you love me.		
7	We need to talk.		
8	How could you do this to me?		

Exercise 2 – Changing behaviour

This exercise has been designed to help you consider your relationship responsibilities and identify any unhelpful behaviour. It is about solving any problems of imbalance and negotiating better ways of working together. Learning new behaviours and breaking bad habits can be difficult, but not impossible. The keys to success are time, practice, and not giving up. The main principle here is to understand each other better, not to argue. Avoid unhelpful Parent–Child discussions.

> Before you start this exercise, it is important to keep in mind that no one can change anyone else's behaviour if they are not willing. But if you change your own behaviour, you may well get a different response.

Materials required

- Paper and pen or pencil

- Traffic light cards

Instructions

☺ *Working alone*

1. Read through the following list of relationship responsibilities.

Heading	Activities
Financial	Paying bills, looking after the money
Domestic	Doing the housework, choosing the furniture/decor, DIY, gardening, cooking
Social	Going out, having friends to visit, choosing what to watch on TV, at the cinema, theatre, etc.
Children	Looking after them, choosing schools, playing with them
Family	Visiting, taking care of relatives, buying Christmas/birthday presents
Sex	Deciding when and where you have sex or what you do

2. Write down the six headings from the above list, and any others you can think of, on a piece of paper.

3. Against each of the items you have listed, write Parent, Adult or Child to indicate how you behave in relation to your relationship responsibilities.

   - Remember you are trying to identify habitual ways of behaving – not temporary behaviours that you might adopt during times of illness, etc.

☯ *Working together*

1. Compare and discuss how you think you behave and relate to each other on these issues.

2. As you discuss the issues, consider which might be the most problematic and answer the following questions in relation to each issue.

   - What attitude or self-defeating behaviours do you want to change in yourself?

   - What will happen if you don't change and continue to do the same things?

   - What will happen if you do change to the new behaviours?

   - What will you have to do to change to new attitudes or behaviours?

   - What obstacles will you have to overcome to maintain the new behaviours?

   - How will you overcome these obstacles?

   - What support do you have for starting new behaviours?

   - What will be your first step in making the change?

   - When will you start to make the changes (date and time)?

   - What reward will you give yourself for your successes?

3. Write down what actions you have agreed to take for each issue you have addressed.

4. Put your list of actions in a prominent place or in your diary so you are reminded of what you have agreed to do.

5. Keep checking back and updating or refining actions.

Use the **PACT** method and **Traffic light cards** to help you avoid conflict.

From the Therapist's Chair

Although the most common cause of divorce nowadays may be cited as 'irreconcilable differences', my experience as a therapist has shown me that many of these differences can be reconciled.

Unfortunately, many couples are so hell-bent on defending their own positions that they can't see how their behaviours are affecting their partners. I frequently hear complaints about partners who are uncooperative or sulk. This type of unhealthy behaviour not only stems from their childhood, but also is often a response to the way they are treated. If you tell someone they are behaving like a child, or treat them like a child, the chances are they will continue to behave like a child.

The Parent–Adult–Child model has helped many couples (even those who have spent years in a state of imbalance) to recognise, understand and change their old habits and unhelpful behaviours.

Points to ponder

- Common myths about love and relationships can influence your expectations and undermine your relationship.

- Power does not breed happiness – holding too much control in a relationship can make you very lonely.

- By manipulating a partner, you will prevent them from ever getting to know or love who you really are.

- Change is scary and 'If it ain't broke, don't fix it' is a common maxim. But if it is 'broke', then change can only be for the better.

Answers to Exercise 1 P–A–C Statements

1. Don't be such a misery. (Parent → Child)

    - Accept and respect your partner's feelings. Ask what has made them unhappy and what you can do to help.

2. You never do anything right. (Parent → Child)

- Be specific and don't blame. Better to say, 'I am not sure why you did/said that. Could you explain?'

3. It's all in your mind – you're imagining it. (Parent → Child)

- Even if your partner is imagining whatever you are being accused of, their fears need addressing, without blame. Ask why they are thinking these things.

4. You're no fun any more. (Child → Parent)

- More blame. This is a partnership – it takes two to have fun. Suggest things to do that you think are fun, and ask them what they would like to do.

5. You don't care about my feelings. (Child → Parent)

- This is an accusation, which is likely to get a defensive response. Talking about your own feelings, using expressions such as 'I feel hurt' can lead to more positive discussion.

6. You never tell me you love me. (Child → Parent)

- Back to blaming. Perhaps 'You often show me that you love me, but I really like to hear it' might get a better result.

7. We need to talk. (Parent → Child)

- These four little words will send most men running for the hills, or at least the potting shed. Be specific and make a request. How about: 'I'd like to talk to you about …'?

8. How could you do this to me? (Child → Parent)

- No matter how wronged you might feel, trying to make someone feel guilty is a form of manipulation. If they already feel guilty, you are rubbing salt into the wound in order to obtain revenge. If they don't, then you are wasting your breath. 'Perhaps you can try to explain why you did it' encourages a more Adult–Adult interaction.

Session 4
Understanding emotions

Our intimate relationships can be a roller-coaster ride of emotions that may take over our lives. When a relationship is good, our happiness may flood into every aspect of our waking thoughts. These positive thoughts and feelings can overcome many of life's difficulties. But when things go wrong, the overwhelming sadness, fear or anger we experience can produce a negative mindset, leading to a vicious circle of negative thinking and unhelpful behaviour.

In order to break a cycle of pain, I try to help couples understand how negative thoughts and emotions can lead to conflict situations. Then I work with them on techniques to help them overcome negative thinking styles, recognise inappropriate negative emotions and express their feelings in a more positive and productive way. Once they gain a better understanding of their own and their partner's feelings, they can overcome emotional barriers, break the cycle of pain and get the supportive reactions they want from each other.

This session starts with some exercises and techniques to help you understand and conquer emotional barriers in your relationship. At the end of the session I have included a short exercise to help you consider male and female differences in emotional expression.

Remember

When you have worked through the exercises in this chapter, review your relationship goals.

Emotions and thoughts

Although our feelings are different from our thoughts, they are inextricably linked: both drive our behaviour. A good example is what is known as the fight-or-flight response. When we experience fear, the emotion triggers chemicals in our bodies to prepare us to either confront the fear (fight) or run away (flight). Once our brains have analysed the threat, we decide on what action to take and behave accordingly. But if our emotions overwhelm us, they can distort our thoughts, which can lead to a misinterpretation of the situation and inappropriate behaviour.

Learning how our own thoughts and emotions interact can help us understand how both we, and our partners, behave in conflict situations. Using a common situation as an example, we can see how thoughts can produce behaviours that instigate a positive reaction.

The situation	*Your partner comes home from work and asks you if you had a good day*
Your feelings	*Happy and relaxed*
Your thoughts	*It is nice to have her/him home*
Your behaviour	*Give them a hug*
Partner's reaction	*Hugs you back*

WHAT IF THE PATTERN GOES LIKE THIS?

The situation	*Your partner comes home from work and doesn't say anything*
Your feelings	*Angry, anxious or worried*
Your thoughts	*What have I done wrong? OR What's wrong with him/her?*
Your behaviour	*Avoid or challenge them*
Partner's reaction	*Ignores you or argues*

In the above example, if you have done something wrong, or know that there is something wrong, your feelings (angry, anxious or worried) could be valid and your thoughts (what have I done wrong?) appropriate. But what if you react this way when there is nothing wrong? To understand why we might react inappropriately in the above situation, we need to consider what happened to us in childhood.

In childhood, for whatever reason, our parents or caregiver might have said, 'You are a bad child – go to your room and don't come out until you know how to behave' or some other such reprimand. We may not remember many such instances, but they will be logged into our unconscious memory. To a child, reprimands can be very frightening (even if they have been naughty). The anxiety a child feels in such a situation can produce thoughts of being unwanted and unloved or rejected, which create negative feelings and distress.

These feelings can be transported into adulthood, even though the situations might be quite different. If our partner ignores us, logically we might know that we are not being rejected. But logic has little to do with our thoughts and reactions if we allow our feelings to overpower us. When we feel anxious or upset, it can be difficult to recognise that our emotions might not necessarily be appropriate to the situation – all we want is to stop feeling bad. To make the bad feelings go away, we might avoid our partner (flight) or behave in a way that creates conflict (fight). By following this pattern, we can get stuck in a cycle of negative or destructive thoughts, emotions and behaviour that can influence all aspects of our relationship.

Breaking the cycle of negative thoughts

In order to break this cycle of unhelpful emotions and unhealthy behaviours, we need to challenge negative thoughts and replace them with alternative explanations.

Applying the previous examples to the table below, we can see how the cycle can be broken. By replacing the negative thoughts in line 3 with the alternative thoughts in line 4, you can change the way you feel (line 5) and behave (line 6). Doing this is likely to get you a positive reaction from your partner (line 7), which will reinforce your feelings about them (line 8).

1 The situation		*Your partner comes home from work and doesn't say anything*
2 Your feelings		*Angry, anxious, worried*
3 Your thoughts		*What have I done wrong?*
4 Your alternative thoughts		*I wonder if they have had a bad day*
5 Your feelings		*Concern*
6 Your behaviour		*Be supportive, tell them you are concerned and ask them if they are OK*
7 Partner's reaction		*Talks to you and tells you about their day*
8 Your feelings		*Warm, sympathetic and loving*

By learning to consider what goes through your mind when things don't go as expected, you will be able to decide if your feelings are appropriate and change your behaviour accordingly.

 Keep in mind that you may not be able to change what goes on in the world but you **can** change the way you think and behave.

Exercise 1 – Emotions and thoughts

In this exercise you will be able to complete your own Emotions and Thoughts Worksheet, which will enable you to explore your own feelings and thoughts and change your behaviour. You do not have to discuss or share your findings from this exercise with your partner. If you do, remember to use the discussion methods you have learned.

Materials required

- Emotions and Thoughts Worksheet (you will find two copies at the end of this session)

Instructions

☺ *Working alone*

1. Recall a moment when you experienced an event that produced an intense emotion: it could have been something that really happened or that you expected to happen. The event might have been brought about by you or by your partner.

   - Try to recall as many details as possible that are pertinent to the chosen emotional episode.

   - This should be **one** (and only one) very specific event that happened recently, preferably within the previous week. It is very important to use a recent event, not a past issue.

2. When you have identified the event, complete the **Emotions and Thoughts Worksheet** in the following way:

1	The situation	*When the situation occurred (day and time), who was involved, what was happening and where it happened*
2	Your feelings	*What you were feeling at the time*
3	Your thoughts	*The thoughts that were going through your mind*
4	Your behaviour	*How you behaved*
5	Partner's reaction	*How your partner reacted to your behaviour*
6	Your feelings	*Your feelings as a result of your partner's reaction*

7	Your alternative thoughts	*An alternative explanation for your partner's behaviour in the situation you have identified in line 1*
8	Your alternative feelings	*Your feelings based on the alternative explanation*
9	Your alternative behaviour	*What you would have done if you had felt this way*
10	Partner's alternative reaction	*How your partner would have reacted to your alternative behaviour*
11	Your feelings	*How you would have felt if your partner had reacted to you in this way*

Understanding the interactions between our emotions and thoughts takes time and practice. Use the Emotions and Thoughts Worksheet for every situation you encounter that produces strong emotions (negative or positive) in the future. By practising this exercise, you will be able to develop the skills to change the thoughts that cause you unnecessary distress and interfere with your relationship.

Saying it with feeling

Since we use complex language, facial expressions and body language to express our emotions, there are endless ways we can mess up our intimate communications.

For example, if you tell your partner they never pay you any attention, does this mean that they are actually ignoring you, or is it because you feel bad about yourself? Sometimes people make such comments because they may be feeling:

- lonely – don't have much to do or don't have many friends;

- unloved – jealous of the attention being given to children, family, friends or work;

- unattractive – lost or put on weight, or the ravages of age are taking their toll;

- insecure – had previous relationships that failed and are frightened it will happen again.

Taking the guesswork out of your emotional communication means under-standing and stating your thoughts and feelings as clearly and positively as you can. There is nothing to be gained from being vague or expecting your partner to have telepathic abilities. It is a complete fallacy to think, '*If my partner loved me he/she would know what I think, mean or feel.*' To expect your partner to know, notice or guess what you want, and then to complain if they don't, is only going to make you feel neglected and leave your partner confused.

Exercise 2 – Saying it with feeling

In Exercise 3 you will be talking about upsetting events that are likely to rekindle strong, unhelpful emotions. Before you start, I have provided this exercise for you to practise discussing emotional topics of a less personal nature. But don't forget to use: the **PACT** discussion method – to stick to the topic; **'I' statements** – to use positive communications; and **traffic light cards** – to avoid arguments.

Materials required

- List of emotions (see overleaf)

- Clock or timer

- Traffic light cards

Instructions

☺ *Working alone*

Think of a topic that you feel strongly about (for example, animal cruelty, child poverty, political/education/employment/health service inadequacies, division of wealth).

- It might help if you write it down.

☯ *Working together*

1. Place this book between you and your partner so that you can both see the list of emotions.

2. Check the time and begin talking about your topic.

   - Allow no more than **10 minutes** to discuss a topic.

3. Use as many words or phrases as you can from the list of emotions to help you express your feelings about your chosen topic.

4. When you have finished, allow your partner to talk about their chosen topic.

LIST OF EMOTIONS

Affectionate	Afraid	Agitated	Amazed
Angry	Anguished	Annoyed	Anxious
Ashamed	Bored	Calm	Carefree
Cheerful	Compassionate	Confident	Confused
Contented	Curious	Dejected	Delighted
Depressed	Desperate	Despondent	Disappointed
Discontented	Discouraged	Disgruntled	Disgusted
Dismayed	Distressed	Doubtful	Eager
Earnest	Ecstatic	Elated	Embarrassed
Embittered	Enthusiastic	Envious	Exasperated
Excited	Exuberant	Fascinated	Fed up
Forlorn	Frightened	Furious	Gloomy
Grateful	Grief-stricken	Guilty	Happy
Hateful	Helpless	Hesitant	Hopeful
Hopeless	Horrified	Hostile	Humble
Impatient	Impressed	Indifferent	Indignant
Inspired	Interested	Jealous	Joyful
Jubilant	Listless	Lively	Lonely
Loving	Melancholic	Nervous	Nostalgic
Offended	Outraged	Passionate	Proud
Regretful	Relaxed	Relieved	Repelled
Resigned	Sad	Satisfied	Scared
Serene	Shy	Sorry	Surprised
Tender	Tense	Touched	Triumphant
Troubled	Uneasy	Unhappy	Worried

 Exercise 3 – Discussing conflict

In this exercise you will be expressing your thoughts and feelings about an area of conflict between you and your partner, or between you and a close relative or friend. To make sure your discussion doesn't become one more episode in whatever unresolved conflicts you have, remember to use: the **PACT** discussion method – to stick to the topic; **'I' statements** – to use positive communications; and **traffic light cards** – to avoid arguments.

Materials required

- List of emotions

- Clock or timer

- Traffic light cards

Instructions

☺ *Working alone*

Think of a recent event that upset you – preferably one that happened within the past few days.

- This could be an event that you have written about in your Emotions and Thoughts Worksheet that happened between you and your partner, or something that happened between you and a member of your family or a friend.

- It might help if you write it down.

☯ *Working together*

1. Place the list of emotions between you and your partner.

2. Check the time and begin talking about your event.

   - Allow no more than **10 minutes** to discuss an event.

3. Use as many words or phrases as you can from the list of emotions to help you express your feelings.

4. When you have finished, allow your partner to talk about their chosen event.

Women vs men – equal but different

In Western societies, boys and girls are usually encouraged to express themselves in different ways. In general, men tend to express their emotions in similar ways to other men, and women in similar ways to other women. Even so, each individual has, to a greater or lesser extent, what may be regarded as both feminine and masculine characteristics. This means that whether your partner is a man or a woman their emotional style could be predominantly either feminine or masculine.

While it is generally believed that men are less emotional than women, it is important to note that we are all able to feel the same emotions. We just don't necessarily feel them about the same things, at the same time, with the same intensity, or express them in the same way.

In relationship therapy, one difference that appears to cause most problems is the way in which couples communicate and express their emotions. Generally, women (and men with more feminine styles of communication) like to hear how their partners feel about them, while men (and women with more masculine styles) like to show how they feel with actions.

UNDERSTANDING WOMEN

In stating that women prefer to talk, I am aware that many of the men reading this are going to be thinking, 'No kidding!' But it's important to realise that for most females the spoken word is the key to all understanding. Women tend to be better than men at reading people, using language, and expressing emotions.

Men often complain to me that they don't understand what women want or expect of them, or how to respond. Let's look at a question often given as an example by men to explain their difficulties in understanding women:

'Does my bum look big in this?'

Superficially, this appears to be a simple question that requires a 'No' or 'Yes' response. But, it could also mean:

Literally

- Do you think I'm fat?

Metaphorically

- I'm feeling neglected. Can you pay me some more attention, please?

- Do you still love me?

- Do you still find me attractive?

- Do you still want to make love to me?

A good answer to this question might be:

'I love your bum – do you think I have been neglecting it recently?'

The only 'secrets' to understanding women are:

- Recognise that they are more likely than men to express their emotions verbally.

- Don't dismiss their need to talk because you can't think of anything emotional to say.

- Admit it when you don't understand what they say and ask them what they mean.

UNDERSTANDING MEN

For men, actions often speak louder than words. Men tend to show their affection by bringing gifts, working hard to pay the bills or fixing something, as well as in other physical ways like touching, hugging, kissing or sex. Unfortunately, since women like to be told they are loved, these physical displays of affection are often misinterpreted.

For example, women often complain that their male partners are only interested in sex because they constantly touch, pat or grab some part of their anatomy. This isn't surprising since physical contact is part of sexual expression. But if you consider that men express their emotions differently, then they might just be trying to say:

- I like the feel of your body;

- I want to be close to you;

- I love you;

- I care about you;

- I find you sexy;

- I enjoy making love with you;

- I want to make love with you whenever you are ready.

The only 'secrets' to understanding men are:

- Recognise that they are more likely than women to express their emotions with actions.

- Don't dismiss all men's actions as sexual intent.

- If you say, '*We need to talk*' they are likely to think they are in trouble and run away in terror.

 Exercise 4 – Equal but different

This exercise is to help you understand the way you both believe you are showing your love for each other and, if necessary, make some changes.

Materials required

- Paper and pen or pencil

Instructions

☺ *Working alone*

1. Write five things you say or do to show your partner you love them.

2. Write five things you would like your partner to do or say to show they love you.

☯ *Working together*

1. Exchange lists and discuss the things you have both written.

2. Agree and make a list of what you want or would like more of.

3. Put your lists in a prominent place to remind you to maintain your agreed actions.

Use the **PACT** discussion method and **traffic light cards** (if necessary).

From the Therapist's Chair

The people I work with in therapy usually arrive in highly emotional states and tend to react to each other without thinking. Their instant retorts and sharp words result in tit-for-tat sequences, which commonly occur in unhappy relationships. Once people begin to recognise that their emotional responses might be more about their own negative thoughts than what their partner says or does, they can begin to break the destructive cycle of pain.

However, understanding negative thought processes isn't going to resolve problems if you are unable to appropriately express your emotions. I know I am beginning to sound like a broken record, but your partner really is only going to know how you feel if you talk to them. I realise that most of the women reading this will be nodding in agreement while many men will be 'expertly' avoiding the idea. So my plea to women with male partners is to be patient and remember that for men actions often speak louder than words. For the male readers it is important to remember that acting like an ostrich and sticking your head in the sand to avoid problems will only result in getting your butt kicked (metaphorically speaking, of course).

Points to ponder

- What we say or do doesn't always tell others how we feel.

- When negative thoughts or emotions occur, ask yourself if there is an alternative explanation.

- The only person you can really change is yourself – but if you change your behaviour you will definitely get a different reaction.

- When talking about difficult topics, it is important to be brief, specific, positive, and have respect for your partner's feelings.

✂ ....

EMOTIONS AND THOUGHTS WORKSHEET

1	The situation	
2	Your feelings	
3	Your thoughts	
4	Your behaviour	
5	Partner's reaction	
6	Your feelings	
7	Your alternative thoughts	
8	Your alternative feelings	
9	Your alternative behaviour	
10	Partner's alternative reaction	
11	Your feelings	

✂ ....

EMOTIONS AND THOUGHTS WORKSHEET

1	The situation	
2	Your feelings	
3	Your thoughts	
4	Your behaviour	
5	Partner's reaction	
6	Your feelings	
7	Your alternative thoughts	
8	Your alternative feelings	
9	Your alternative behaviour	
10	Partner's alternative reaction	
11	Your feelings	

Session 5
Romance

Many therapists and self-help books tend to assume that when couples resolve their conflicts, the romance will return to their relationship. Yet I have worked with couples in therapy where a lack of romance *was* the problem. When romance disappears from a relationship, couples often become dissatisfied, with the result that even the smallest of problems can become a major issue.

Romance is the fun part of a relationship. When we first meet our partners, the novelty, mystery, uncertainty and anticipation add excitement. After the relationship is established, we tend to settle into the comfort of familiarity and security, and so the excitement can easily fade. It can seem difficult to know how to recapture the excitement, particularly when there have been problems. Although we can't expect our lives to be like a Hollywood movie, everyone needs a little excitement in their life to combat the monotony of day-to-day living.

Having worked your way through the first four sessions of this book, you should now be ready to put some romance back into your relationship. At this stage of your DIY therapy, the focus is on re-establishing and improving the fun and passion. Don't worry if you haven't completely resolved all your conflicts. It takes time and practice to hone your relationship skills – and a little romance will help.

 All you need to do now is:

- have the desire to create special times with your partner;

- be open to more possibilities;

- allow ideas to flow;

- take some risks;

- have some fun.

Keeping romance alive

So what romantic things can you do to make your relationship more alive? That depends on you and your partner. Romance is not a case of 'one size fits all' – even the roses, candles and chocolates can get boring.

You might not consider yourself to be romantic, or perhaps you feel you haven't the confidence to show your romantic side. Even worse, you might think you are too old for romance. Perhaps the following story will help:

> *Some years ago, when my parents had been married for over 50 years, my mother was admitted to hospital. Since she didn't like the hospital food, my father brought her meals from home. Hidden underneath the plate of one of the meals was a love note. This was from a man who is naturally shy and reserved, who grew up at a time when 'men were men' and romance was for poets and women.*

If you want to be more romantic but lack the confidence, try to avoid thinking that romance is something artificial that you must 'do', or that it requires big, expensive gestures. Instead, think about romance merely as a means of expressing your love in ways that your partner will enjoy.

The basic message is that you don't have to be a romantic to be romantic. If you make an effort to give romance a chance, you can put the fun and passion back into your relationship.

BEFORE YOU START

Being romantic isn't about doing what's expected or trying to impress. For example, which of the following do you consider are the most romantic?

- Someone who buys their partner a present on their birthday.
  - While this is nice, it is rather predictable – not romantic as such.
- A person who buys their partner a present, just because they feel like it.
  - This is much better. It expresses a 'just because I love you' moment.
- A person who *makes* their partner a present – just because …
  - This is even better. It shows that thought, time and effort have been put into the gift.

If you want more romance but your partner doesn't seem to be romantic, don't constantly remind them of their 'failings'. Encourage them by being romantic yourself. Start with little ways and see what happens.

 ## Exercise 1 – Special someone

Being romantic means making your partner feel special. If you don't know by now what your partner likes, what they enjoy and what gets them excited, it's time that you did! By demonstrating that you know what makes them unique, you are more able to make them feel special.

Important

 Mind reading is one of the biggest threats to a relationship; so don't make assumptions. Even if you think you know what they like, it is always good to check – they might have changed their minds.

Materials required

- Paper and pen or pencil

Instructions

☺ *Working alone*

Write your answers to the following questions:

- What is your partner interested in; for example, their hobbies, what they read, watch on TV, etc.?

- What makes their eyes light up; for example, when they're shopping, watching a movie, or reading?

- What could you do for your partner that only they would appreciate?

- What could you say to compliment them that only they would like?

Working together

1. Check your answers with your partner and see if these are the things they like.

2. Ask them what else they like; for example, their favourite colours, places, clothes, their preferred times for making love, etc …

Learning to play together

As we grow into adulthood and get into a 'serious' relationship, we often forget how to have fun and just be silly. When the couples I work with in therapy learn or remember how to play together, they are often able to overcome many of their problems. Of course, this doesn't mean that their problems disappear simply because they are having fun together. But adult play and fun is important because it can:

-   develop imagination, creativity and problem solving skills;

-   attune us to each other;

-   enhance our sense of belonging and reinforce trust;

-   enable us to satisfy our curiosity and explore in a non-threatening way.

For these reasons, it's not difficult to see how play and romance go hand-in-hand. Play encourages us to be imaginative, open and trusting, which are all key ingredients of romance.

> **Important**
>
> ❗ Playtime isn't just for children. It is fundamental in an intimate relationship; so keep this one point in mind:
>
> **Adult play is essential for personal health and relationship success.**

The following pages contain some ideas for romance and play that have helped couples in therapy rekindle that 'loving feeling'.

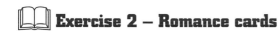 Exercise 2 – Romance cards

To help couples in therapy reignite the flame of romance and put a little fun back into their relationships, I compiled two sets of 'cards': one set contains topics for conversation, which helps couples find something to talk about apart from work, home, children, etc., and the other contains ideas for activities to try. At the end of face-to-face therapy sessions I provide couples with a small random selection of cards for use between sessions. To help them recapture the excitement of a new relationship I add a little uncertainty by supplying the cards in sealed envelopes with specific instructions on when to open them.

At the end of this session you will find tables containing some of the topics for conversations and ideas for activities, similar to the cards I use with couples in therapy. Below are the instructions on how to use them to add excitement to your DIY therapy.

Materials required

- Conversations and Activities Tables (you will find these at the end of this session)

- Scissors

- Two small boxes

    - Sandwich boxes with lids will allow you to shake up the cards and make a random selection.

Instructions

1. Cut out the pages containing tables marked 'Romantic Conversations' and 'Romantic Activities'.

2. Cut out each square in the tables to make your own cards and put them in the boxes, one marked 'Conversations' and one marked 'Activities'.

    - Do not remove any you think are silly, pointless or not the sort of thing you might say or do. Remember, romance is about uncertainty and mystery. If nothing else, they will give you something to laugh about.

3. You might also wish to add some ideas of your own, but do bear in mind that this is about romance; there are tables later in the book containing conversations and activities to help you put some fun back into your sex lives.

Remember

Romance is about novelty and surprise. But don't forget to use the communication skills you have learned and **do not** rush the activities. Take time to have fun with romance and see where it takes you both.

Using your romance cards

Couples in therapy usually agree to participate in homework exercises, some of which involve the use of the romance cards. The romance cards have been designed for use with the exercises that follow, or whenever you and your partner have time alone together, without the usual interruptions of family, friends, television, etc.

Using the Activity and Conversation Cards

1. Shake up the Activities box, select one card each and do what it says.

    - If that particular activity isn't possible at the time you select it (for example, the card instructs you to spend a day at the seaside and play on the fairground), replace it or put it to one side for later use, and select another card.

2. Shake up the Conversations box and select one card.

3. Discuss a topic from one side of the card until you have exhausted that topic.

4. Give the card to your partner to talk about the topic on the reverse of the card.

 Exercise 3 – Dating

Just because you are living together doesn't mean you can't date! Remember that when you first met, the excitement came from your preparation for the date: deciding what to wear, the anticipation of not knowing what was going to happen and what you might say or do. In therapy, I recommend that couples have at least one 'date' every two weeks and that each partner takes it in turn to arrange the dates.

The first two dating ideas are entitled 'Staying in Dates' and 'Going out Dates'. These are followed by another two, entitled 'Strangers' Meeting' and 'Role Play', which might appear a little bizarre. These dates allow couples in therapy to explore something new, take a few risks and let go of their inhibitions. As your DIY therapist, I strongly encourage you to lay down the mantle of adult responsibility and enjoy some playtime.

Important

If you are arranging a 'date', don't forget that you have to make all the arrangements and do all the preparation and clearing up. This will ensure that your partner feels special and relaxed.

Staying in dates

You don't need to go out or spend a lot of money to have a date. Staying in can provide a very intimate setting in which you can have fun.

Materials required

- Conversation and activity cards

Instructions

1. Tell your partner you would like to have a special evening, morning or afternoon at home alone together – agree the day and time.

2. Set the scene – prepare the room and food, etc. Try to think of something new to do with your partner, something you haven't done before, for instance:

   - Prepare/cook an entire meal, making it special with table settings, flowers, candles.

   - Make a bowl of popcorn and curl up on the sofa together to watch a romantic movie.

   - Picnic together on the rug in front of the fire, or in the garden.

   - Prepare some snacks and play a board game you haven't played for years.

3. Make sure you are not disturbed. Turn off the computer, television and telephone and, if you have children, put them to bed or get a friend or relative to look after them.

4. Use the Activity and Conversation cards to add a little fun on your date.

Going out dates

This must be a real 'date' – not just going out together to the usual places.

Materials required

- Conversation and activity cards

Instructions

1. Tell your partner you would like to go out with them on a particular day and at a specific time. Be prepared to negotiate.

    - Try to think of something new to do with your partner, something you haven't done before or for a long time.

2. Make *all* the arrangements (including childcare if necessary).

    - Take some Conversation and Activity Cards (without looking at them) to add some surprises to your date.

3. When you get home, don't go straight to bed – make your partner a drink and chat, or sit and have a cuddle on the sofa.

Strangers' meeting

To add a little more excitement to your dates you could try something a bit different.

Materials required

- Conversation and Activity Cards

Instructions

1. Tell your partner you would like to go out with them on a particular day and at a specific time. Be prepared to negotiate.

2. Decide on a meeting place and either:

    - tell them the time and place of the meeting, *or*

    - to add a little more mystery and excitement, don't tell them beforehand where you are going to meet but telephone them when you get there.

3. Get ready alone: enjoy the preparation and don't let your partner see what you are wearing.

    - Take some Conversation and Activity Cards (without looking at them) to add some surprises to your date.

4. When your partner arrives, make the first approach, as though you were approaching someone you are trying to 'pick up'.

   - The aim is to engage your partner to get them to spend the rest of the evening with you.

5. When you have succeeded (and you will), you can take them on to whatever you have planned.

Role play dates

This is a variation of the 'going out date', but with a little added excitement of pretending to be different people. Some couples in therapy change their appearances subtly, using elegant evening dress to be a James Bond and a Miss Moneypenny, for instance. Others have used elaborate or outrageous fancy dress to assume different roles and show a more adventurous side of their personalities. Though this type of date is not for the faint-hearted, the couples who have tried it have had lots of fun.

Materials required

- Conversation and Activity Cards

- Fancy dress

Instructions

1. Tell your partner you would like to go out with them on a particular day and at a specific time. Be prepared to negotiate.

   - Make *all* the arrangements (including childcare if necessary).

   - Take some Conversation and Activity Cards each (without looking at them) to use on your date.

2. Get ready alone: enjoy the preparation and don't let your partner see what you are wearing. Below are a few ideas that couples in therapy have used, which you might try – if you dare!

   - Wear a fashion from your youth or when you first met (for example, hippy, mod, rocker, punk, goth, etc.) and be that young again.

   - Turn up in fancy dress (for example, teddy bear meets cowboy).

   - Dress and act like your favourite film character (for example, Indiana Jones meets Lara Croft).

From the Therapist's Chair

When couples put romance back into their relationship, they have a different perspective on many of their conflicts. They are better able to view their problems in a more united and creative way and find solutions that are meaningful to them.

At this stage in therapy, I am constantly amazed not only at the change in the way couples are able to communicate but also at their capacity to have fun. Their inventiveness in the cards they create for themselves and the characters they use for their role play dates are a continuous source of joy. I am grateful to all those I have worked with who have allowed me into their world of fun.

The exercises in this session have helped many couples add romance, play and fun into their relationship and have been beneficial in enhancing their sex lives. The following sessions address sexual problems and include exercises, activities and more DIY therapy cards designed to help you boost your sex lives.

Points to ponder

- Adults need play – it makes them and their relationships happy and healthy.

- Romantic play reinforces intimate bonds and strengthens trust.

- Being romantic means using your imagination and being creative.

- Making your partner feel special is the secret of romance; the excitement of romance can be rekindled with a little mystery.

✂ ROMANTIC CONVERSATION CARDS

Ask your partner about their favourite date the two of you shared.	*What are you proudest of about yourself? Why?*
Compliment your partner on how nice they look or something they have achieved.	*What is you favourite smell, when, where and how did you discover it?*
Describe a happy holiday memory from any period of your life.	*What is your favourite place in the world?*
Describe a recent occasion when you felt truly happy. What was it that made you feel so good?	*What is your favourite taste/food?*
Describe an experience that was so much fun you wanted it to last for ever.	*What is your favourite television programme? Why do you like it?*
Describe the ways in which your partner has become more attractive since you first met.	*What is your ideal of a perfect day? What time of year would it be; what would the weather be like and what would you do?*

Describe one way in which you would like to be pampered.

What item of clothing do you really enjoy wearing? Explain why.

Describe something funny that has happened in your family.

What new hobbies or leisure pursuits would you like to try? Explain why.

Describe something romantic that you would like to do with your partner.

What pet, or other animals, do you particularly like?

Describe three people (living or dead) who would be your ideal guests at a party.

What risks would you like to take in the future?

How would you change the world, in a big or small way?

What was the first movie you saw?

If you could choose any country to live in, which one would it be and why?

What was the job you thought you would like when you were a child?

If you were a car, which car would you be and why?	*What was the naughtiest thing you did when you were growing up?*
If you were an animal, what kind of animal would you like to be and why?	*What was your first alcoholic drink, when and where did you drink it?*
If you were a type of food, which food would you be and why?	*What would you like to spend more time doing by yourself and why?*
Name a piece of music and explain what memories it stimulates.	*What would you like to spend more time doing with your partner?*
If you were a country, which country would you be and why?	*What would you like to do that you haven't already done?*
Talk about your favourite music. Explain how it makes you feel.	*When you were a child, what did you want to be when you grew up?*

Tell your partner about one of the romantic moments you have previously shared.	*Where else might you like to live and how is it different from where you live now?*
Tell your partner one reason why you love them.	*Where would be your favourite holiday destination? Why?*
Tell your partner three things that you find attractive about him/her.	*Which famous person from any period of history would you like to be? Why?*
Tell your partner about a recent time when they made you feel special.	*Who has been a major influence in your life? Describe the ways this person has affected you.*
Tell your partner how good they made you feel when …	*Who is your favourite film star or celebrity, why do you like them, what do you admire?*
What are you proudest of about your partner? Why?	*Who was your very first 'best' friend? How and when did you meet, what was your relationship like?*

✂ ROMANTIC ACTIVITIES CARDS

Arrange a day at the seaside and play on the fairground.	*Make a date to go swimming wearing your sexiest costumes.*
Arrange a joint pampering day at a health spa.	*Make a surprise visit to your partner's workplace for coffee or lunch.*
Bake a cake together.	*Make your partner a drink that you know they like.*
Book a day at a sporting event.	*Make your partner their favourite dessert.*
Buy something silly for each other.	*Offer to do (or help with) the shopping.*
Close your eyes and explore your partner's face with your fingertips.	*Paint your partner's toenails.*

Do something to make your partner laugh.	*Pick your partner a bunch of wild flowers.*
Drive to a local beauty spot, park the car, cuddle, kiss and cuddle.	*Plan and book an outing, weekend or holiday together.*
During the next meal (alone) swap genders.	*Send your partner an email with a photograph of the two of you attached.*
Feed each other (as you would a small child) for half of the next meal.	*Play 'your' song and ask your partner to dance with you.*
Gently kiss the back of your partner's neck.	*Play your favourite piece of music for your partner and tell them what you like about it.*
Give your partner a foot massage.	*Prepare your partner a luxury bath, with foam and candles or rubber ducks.*

Give your partner a hand massage.

Put on some music and sing along with it together (air guitar optional).

Give your partner a hug and kiss them on the forehead.

Set up a 'love snack' with food your partner likes and feed him/her.

Give your partner a neck massage.

Stroke your partner's hand when sitting across the dinner table and tell them how much you love them.

Give your partner a peck on the cheek.

Stroke your partner's hair.

Give your partner an anniversary card on any day that is not your anniversary.

Take your partner to the local children's playground and play on the swings.

Give your partner a back/shoulder massage.

Take your partner breakfast in bed.

Go for a walk after dark and feed the ducks in a local park.

Take your partner to the country or seaside for a picnic.

Go window shopping when the shops are closed, stopping in shop doorways for some kisses.

Telephone or text your partner and tell them you are thinking of them.

Help your partner on/off with their coat and give them a hug.

The next time you walk past your partner gently stroke your fingers across their back.

Hold your partner's hand when you are out walking together.

Use your partner's name often.

Kiss your partner gently and softly on their eyelids, nose and lips.

Watch the sunset together at a local beauty spot.

Leave your partner a note telling them you love them.

Write your partner a love letter.

Session 6
Let's talk about sex

In Session 2, 'Identifying the Problems', I briefly explained, in a short section 'A Word about Sex', that relationship and sexual problems usually go hand-in-hand. For this reason, couples with sexual difficulties are asked to refrain from sex (and from talking about sex) until relationship difficulties have been resolved. When this has been achieved, couples often feel ready and eager to resume their sexual activities. But they are usually surprised, and more than a little disappointed, when I ask them to maintain the sex 'taboo'. This ban on sex is a vital part of sex therapy since it serves a number of functions. Sex needs to be off the menu to start with so that neither partner feels under pressure to perform, until they are able to:

- talk about sex without confusion;

- identify if there are any physical problems;

- understand their own and their partner's sexual responses.

Couples are then better able to trust each other with their bodies. They will have the confidence to begin to explore and refine their sexual techniques as well as to experiment with new experiences.

The focus of this session and the four that follow is on physical intimacy. The methods included have been based on the revolutionary work of Masters and Johnson in the 1960s. Their approach focused on providing information to increase sexual knowledge, along with behavioural exercises to develop new skills. The effectiveness of these methods is evidenced by the fact that individuals and couples have successfully used them for over half a century. In addition, in order to add an extra dimension of fun and relaxation, I have included some of my own methods – all of which have been tried and tested with clients.

Sexually speaking

Talking about sex can be difficult. One of the main reasons couples don't talk about sex is simply through habit. When we first meet someone, explicit conversations about sex are not really appropriate. So when sex is first initiated, we tend to fumble around and try to guess what our partner likes. Having heard a few moans that we interpret as appreciation, we just carry on, assuming we must be doing it right. As time passes, unless we really communicate at an intimate level, the habits set in. But old habits can get boring, as well as hard to break.

Most of the people I see in therapy are fairly well educated and articulate, yet they seem to be unable to 'really talk' to their partners about sex, even when there is a problem. Previously, I mentioned that part of my role as a therapist involves being a 'mediator', helping couples to effectively deal with their relationship issues. Within the sex domain I view myself as more of a 'translator', ensuring that couples are speaking the same language. What I mean by this is helping them develop a 'sexual language' they feel comfortable with in order to understand each other's sexual wants and needs.

The following exercises have been designed to help you talk about sex before you discuss any sexual problems or begin the 'sexercises' included in the following sessions.

Exercise 1 – Sexual truths and half-truths

When we are children, if we are lucky, our parents might tell us some basic facts of reproduction. Sex education at school rarely provides much more. As teenagers we learn what other teenagers think you are 'supposed' to do, which is often fuelled by the media, popular magazines and (for some) pornography.

Despite the bombardment of sexual references and images we are subjected to nowadays, it is a moot point whether we are much the wiser. Unfortunately, much of the information we receive about sex is far from reliable and often misunderstood. Take movies, for example, where the first sexual encounter between couples is usually portrayed as a perfect union of perfect bodies achieving simultaneous orgasm. True to life? I don't think so.

In this exercise you are provided with a questionnaire containing 20 commonly held beliefs about sex, with brief explanations at the end of the session.

Materials required

- Traffic light cards

Instructions

☯ *Working together*

1. Discuss each of the following statements in the grid below.

2. Place a cross in the appropriate column against each statement to indicate if you and your partner believe the statement is 'mostly true' or 'mostly false'.

   - If you do not agree on an answer, use your initials to indicate which one of you believes the statement is 'mostly true' and which one thinks it is 'mostly false'.

3. Check your answers against the explanations at the end of the session.

	Statement	Mostly true	Mostly false
1	Everyone else is having more sex than me/us.		
2	If you don't achieve orgasm, you should fake it.		
3	Masturbation is not normal in a good sexual relationship.		
4	Oral sex is bad or wrong.		
5	People who are ill or disabled aren't able to have sex.		
6	People who have sexual fantasies are not happy with their partners.		
7	Sex drive diminishes with age.		
8	Sex is 'dirty'.		
9	Sex is satisfying only if you have an orgasm.		
10	Sex should be spontaneous.		
11	The best sex ends in simultaneous orgasm with your partner.		
12	There is no place for erotica or pornography in a relationship.		
13	You should always be in the mood for sex.		
14	A man with a large penis is better able to satisfy a partner.		
15	Men are only interested in sex.		
16	Men should know how to please their partners.		
17	To have sex a man must have a full erection.		
18	A woman should be able to have an orgasm during intercourse alone.		
19	Women have a lower sex drive than men.		
20	Women should wait for men to initiate sex.		

Exercise 2 – Sexual language

There is a considerable amount of research that shows people (including health professionals) often find it difficult to talk about sex. This is often because we are embarrassed, which can result in not being able to find the right words to express ourselves clearly. For example, if a patient tells their doctor they have a pain in their bum, are they talking about their gluteus maximus or their anus?

The things we say to our partners can convey the wrong message and turn them on or off to sex. Consider the following:

'Fancy a shag?' vs. 'Would you like to make love?'

'You have beautiful breasts' vs. 'I love your tits.'

Although both versions of these two messages express more or less the same thing, there is a world of difference between them. Before you start to talk about sex, it is important that you agree on the language that is clear and acceptable to both of you.

This exercise will help you think about the language you use when talking about sex. Remember to continue using DIY therapy communication skills (the **PACT** model and **'I' statements**).

Materials required

- Paper and pen or pencil

- Traffic light cards (if necessary)

Instructions

☺ *Working alone*

For each of the following, write the words or phrases:

- your partner uses to describe them;

- what you would like your partner to use to describe them.

Anus	Anal sex	Arousal	Breasts	Clitoris
Desire	Erection	Foreplay	Intercourse	Masturbation
Oral sex	Orgasm	Penis	Testicles	Vagina

☯ Working together

Discuss each item and agree the things that you both feel comfortable saying when you are talking about sex with each other.

- If you prefer to use different words while in the throes of passion, these should also be acceptable to both of you.

 # Exercise 3 – Things we like

By the time we get into a sexual relationship, we embark on a journey of trial and error filled with erroneous expectations that can produce anxieties and create problems. It takes time and experience to decide what is right for us as individuals.

Many people make assumptions about what their partners enjoy without actually asking them and can be too embarrassed to tell their partners what they enjoy. This exercise is designed to help you and your partner discuss in an open and honest way the good and not so good things in your sex lives.

In this exercise you will be talking about the sexual things you like to do with your partner. Don't forget to use the **PACT** model and **'I' statements**.

Materials required

- Traffic light cards

Instructions

☯ Working together

Take it in turns to tell your partner:

- one thing you like about your sexual activities, why and how much you like it;

- something different you would like to do or try;

- something that you would like to change.

From the Therapist's Chair

 I firmly believe that if couples could talk to each other more openly about sex, they would have fewer problems and there would be less need for therapy. Problems can occur because couples are unable, or unwilling, to discuss their issues. They can also occur when people make assumptions about what their partner wants, needs or thinks. A good example of this is provided by the following case.

John and Jane, who had been married for 30 years, came to see me to enquire if John could take oral medication for his erectile dysfunction. John had undergone heart surgery and was on a cocktail of prescribed medication, which meant that oral medication was unlikely to be suitable. Before discussing the possible options available to John, I asked him if he wanted to be able to get an erection and, if so, why. He revealed that he wasn't really bothered but he was worried Jane might leave him if he couldn't 'perform like a man'. Before I could respond, Jane said that she wasn't bothered about intercourse, explaining that she was very happy with the way things were. But she had been worried that if John couldn't get an erection, he would be unhappy.

Having discussed their issues, John and Jane left their first and last therapy session without medical intervention, happy with their own particular methods of expressing their intimacy.

Points to ponder

- Talking about sex openly, without embarrassment and in a caring, supportive way, can help resolve problems and enhance sexual experiences.

- Using the words your partner prefers to hear helps to avoid confusion and improve sexual response.

- Your partner can only know what you like if you tell them.

Answers to Exercise 1 Sexual truths and half-truths

1. Everyone else is having more sex than me/us.

    - Lots of surveys (both scientific and media based) have been conducted on the number of times people in relationships engage in sexual intercourse. The main problem with all of them is that they rely on what people say, which can be very different from what they actually do. Another problem is that they focus on the quantity of penetrative sex rather than the more important aspect of quality, which might be more satisfying than a 'wham and bang'.

    - For those of you who want some figures, the average frequency of intercourse reported by people in these surveys is from twice a week to once a fortnight. But this is an average of the range from every day (where do they find the time?) to never.

2. If you don't achieve orgasm, you should fake it.

    - Faking orgasm is never a good idea, since it can lead to sexual frustration and relationship problems.

3. Masturbation is not normal in a good sexual relationship.

    - Masturbation is a normal, healthy activity practised by the majority of men and women, including those in sexual relationships.

4. Oral sex is bad or wrong.

    - Many people enjoy oral sex and it is neither bad nor wrong if you and your partner enjoy it. Some women resist their partner's attempts to perform oral sex upon them, believing that their vaginas are dirty, yet there are fewer bacteria in the vagina than in the mouth!

5. People who are ill or disabled aren't able to have sex.

    - Long-term illness or disability does not and should not affect your love life. While some conditions and physical impairments might prevent people from having sexual intercourse, a satisfying intimate relationship can be enjoyed by learning new techniques.

6. People who have sexual fantasies are not happy with their partners.

    - Fantasies, sexual or otherwise, are an enjoyable distraction from the difficulties of life and have little bearing on the way we feel about our partner. Sexual fantasies can help both women and men to get in the mood for sex or to maintain their arousal.

7. Sex drive diminishes with age.

    - If sex drive diminishes, it is more likely to be due to health problems that are associated with ageing rather than a person's age.

8. Sex is 'dirty'.

    - Sex can be messy but never dirty (unless you and your partner don't bathe very often). When people believe sex is dirty, it is usually related to feelings of guilt, often because of negative messages they have received early in their lives.

9. Sex is satisfying only if you have an orgasm.

    - There are many ways to achieve sexual satisfaction, and orgasm is only one of them. Both women and men are capable of enjoying sex without experiencing an orgasm.

10. Sex should be spontaneous.

    - Sexual spontaneity is fine, but rare. People tend to forget all the preparations they made in the anticipation of 'spontaneous' sex in the early stages of their relationship.

11. The best sex ends in simultaneous orgasm with your partner.

    - Having an orgasm at the same time as your partner can be nice but is no guarantee of good sex. Many couples rarely (if ever) manage to achieve simultaneous orgasm.

12. There is no place for erotica or pornography in a relationship.

    - Erotic or pornographic materials, like fantasies, can help people to get in the mood for sex. This does not mean there is a problem either with the person using these stimulants or with their relationship.

13. You should always be in the mood for sex.

    - Sometimes people are in the mood for sex before they start. Sometimes the desire for sex comes only after they have been physically stimulated.

14. A man with a large penis is better able to satisfy a partner.

    - Men often worry about the size of their penis but few men have seen another man's erect penis, except perhaps in an adult movie – and these men are not chosen for their acting abilities! Studies indicate that the average length of a man's erect penis is about 13–15 centimetres (5–6 inches), which is more than ample for an average vagina (7–11 centimetres or $2\frac{1}{2}-4\frac{1}{4}$ inches). Ultimately, sexual satisfaction depends more on technique than penis size.

15. Men are only interested in sex.

   • The popular media tend to promote the idea that men are obsessed with sex, which could have some vestige of truth for young, single men. Men want sex sometimes and not others – just like women. There is a wealth of research that shows that men in relationships are not interested only in sex but also want and enjoy affection. And some research has found that men in long-term heterosexual relationships are often more interested in affection than women.

16. Men should know how to please their partners.

   • It is one thing to know what to do in an abstract sense, but a man (or woman) will only know what to do with a partner if they ask them what they like and want.

17. To have sex a man must have a full erection.

   • Penetration can be achieved with a semi-erect penis. All it takes is a little patience, some lubrication and the right techniques.

18. A woman should be able to have an orgasm during intercourse alone.

   • Women generally need clitoral stimulation to achieve orgasm but there are very few sexual positions where this can be achieved. Most women can only achieve orgasm during intercourse if they, or their partner, use their fingers (or a vibrator) to stimulate the clitoris.

19. Women have a lower sex drive than men.

   • Much of the early research into human sexual behaviour would support this statement. Recent research on brain activity suggests that the male sex drive is more constant, while the female sex drive tends to be periodic but more intense.

20. Women should wait for men to initiate sex.

   • Many men like women who take the initiative and really enjoy themselves in bed.

Session 7
Sexual problems

Sexuality is not an optional extra, since everyone has sexual needs, feelings, desires and drives. The media encourage us to believe that we should all be sexual athletes – and gold medal athletes at that! But what about when the flames of passion die and the urges wane? Well, the good news is that gold medals aren't the aim; it's being in the game that matters, and the game should involve whatever the players enjoy. Even if the mind is willing but the body is weak, there are many ways to relight your flame. The first and most important way to get back in the game is to find out what is holding you back.

Talking therapies can no more mend a broken leg than plaster casts can mend broken hearts or minds. Therefore, when individuals or couples with sexual problems consult a sex therapist, they complete a health check questionnaire to identify if they have a problem that requires medical consultation. Before you continue with your DIY therapy, it is equally important for you to try to identify any problem that requires medical advice.

This session contains information used by therapists when conducting health checks. It covers the types of factors that have been associated with sexual dysfunction, such as lifestyle, medical conditions and medications. Also included are brief descriptions of the most commonly experienced sexual problems treated by sex therapy techniques.

Why is it important to have a health check?

Asking individuals or couples with sexual problems to undertake a health check helps therapists determine two things: first, whether the sexual problem is due to an unhealthy lifestyle or existing medical condition; and, second, whether the sexual dysfunction is an indicator of an undiagnosed medical condition.

This second point has come to light in recent years since cardiovascular specialists realised that erectile dysfunction (an inability to achieve or maintain an erection) can sometimes be an early warning sign for an undetected physical condition. The reason for their particular interest is because the blood that creates the erection is delivered through arteries that are smaller (1–2 millimetres) than the ones in the heart (3–4 millimetres) and neck (5–7 millimetres). Therefore, if a man's penis isn't working, it could be an early sign of a hardening and narrowing of the arteries (atherosclerosis), which can also cause such conditions as heart attacks and strokes. So the penis can be a bit like a barometer, and its rise and fall can help in the early detection of undiagnosed and potentially life-threatening conditions.

In a similar way to men, a woman's ability to become physically aroused (when the vagina becomes engorged with blood and produces lubrication) also relies on a healthy vascular system. However, as yet, there has been little research into female arousal disorder and cardiovascular problems. Since many women are unaware of the more discreet physical changes that take place during sexual excitement, arousal problems are much more difficult to identify.

But whether you are male or female, the bottom line is that if you are unable to be sexual, despite wanting to and getting adequate stimulation, it is worth a visit to your doctor.

Examining your lifestyle

One of the first things to check is whether there is anything about your lifestyle that could be affecting your sexual performance.

There are numerous environmental factors that can occur throughout our lives that are not conducive to sexual activity. At some time in our lives we might have to live in situations that give us little privacy (for example, living with relatives or in cramped accommodation with children). Since time alone with your partner is vital, not only for sexual activity but to maintain the intimate bond you have, it is important to try to find somewhere to be alone, even if it is only for a few hours each month.

The state of one's health can be another factor. For instance, a health problem that has been associated with sexual difficulties is obesity, with morbidly obese people being 25 times more likely than those of normal weight to report problems with their sex lives. This is perhaps not surprising if we consider that obesity contributes to conditions like atherosclerosis, which can affect blood supply to the genitals. However, being overweight is not just a physical issue; it can also affect our body image, reduce sexual confidence and increase anxiety. These additional psychological aspects can result in decreased sexual activity or avoiding sex completely. But since sex is a physical exercise that can help with weight loss and improve circulation, it would be better to include sexual activity in any weight loss programme.

Prolonged periods of stress, which we know to have a damaging effect on the body, can also interfere with sexual activity. Not only that, but some people try to cope through the abuse of substances that help them to relax and unwind, which only adds to the problem. Listed below are a number of recreational substances that have been associated with sexual problems:

- Alcohol

- Amphetamines

- Barbiturates

- Cocaine

- Marijuana

- Methadone

- Nicotine

- Opiates

Medical conditions and medication

Sexual problems can be caused by a large number of medical conditions and also by the drugs prescribed to treat these. For example, people who suffer from depression often have little interest in anything – including sex. Unfortunately, some drugs used to treat depression can reduce sexual desire. It is not uncommon for men with erectile dysfunction to tell their doctors that they are depressed but fail to discuss their sexual difficulties. Consequently, they might be prescribed antidepressants that exacerbate their sexual problems.

So, if you are experiencing sexual problems and have (or suspect you have) a medical condition, or if you are worried about your health, consult your doctor. Also, if you are taking prescribed medication, do not stop taking it without consulting your doctor.

Important

 It is vital that you tell your doctor if you are experiencing a sexual problem.

Below is a list of medical conditions that have been associated with sexual difficulties:

- Cancer (in particular, affecting the pelvis, genitals, bladder, prostate, rectum)

- Chronic fatigue or weakness

- Diabetes (high blood sugar)

- Heart disease (heart attack, chest pain with exercise or sex)

- High blood pressure

- High cholesterol levels

- Hormone problems

- Injury, surgery or radiation treatment (spine, pelvis, genitals, bladder, prostate or rectum)

- Joint pains (severe or chronic problems moving or changing positions)

- Kidney disease

- Neurological problems (Parkinson's disease, multiple sclerosis, spine injury)

- Prostate problems

- Psychological, psychiatric or emotional problems (such as depression, anxiety, schizophrenia)

- Sexually transmitted diseases

- Urinary problems (urgency, frequency, hesitancy, weak stream, infection)

- Vascular disease (stroke, mini stroke, blockage of the arteries, aneurysms)

People with chronic medical conditions (and disabilities) often suffer sexual problems in silence, believing that there are no remedies. However, remedies come in many forms. Even if there are no medical solutions to your particular problem, you can still enjoy a satisfying sexual relationship provided you are willing to try some new techniques.

Sexual problems explained

Most people are likely to experience an occasional sexual problem, which usually passes after a short period of time. However, if you are experiencing a sexual problem that is causing you and/or your partner distress, the first step is to try to identify what the problem is.

Physical problems are usually identified by lack of genital engorgement, lubrication or sensation. They can arise because of an inadequate blood flow or nerve supply to the genitals, due to a medical condition. But lack of sensation can also occur because of poor techniques due to inexperience or an inadequate understanding of our own physical responses and/or those of our partner.

Psychological concerns about body image, as well as a lack of confidence in sexual abilities and techniques, are common anxieties that respond well to methods regularly employed by sex therapists. People with more deep-seated psychological problems (specific phobias, traumas resulting from sexual abuse or rape, etc.) also respond well to sex therapy. However, these are likely to require more specialist help than any book is able to provide.

General relationship difficulties, such as the stresses and strains of daily living and lack of time or privacy, will interfere with the healthiest of sex lives. In addition, poor sexual techniques, being bored with sex or no longer attracted to a partner are frequent reasons given by couples for diminished sexual enjoyment. But a much more common problem is the inability (or unwillingness) to talk about sexual concerns.

Do bear in mind, though, that it is possible to have more than one problem at the same time. For example, it isn't unusual for loss of desire to be experienced in conjunction with other sexual difficulties and dysfunctions. It is also important to recognise that, even if a physical component can be identified, most sexual difficulties are associated with a complex interaction between physical, psychological and relationship difficulties.

The following common sexual problems listed are regularly treated using behavioural techniques, sometimes in conjunction with medical intervention. Read through their brief descriptions and discuss with your partner any that you believe might be affecting your relationship.

LOSS OF SEXUAL DESIRE

Losing the desire for, or interest in, sex (referred to in medical terms as Hypoactive Sexual Desire Disorder) has been described as both the most common and challenging of the sexual problems. It is defined as the persistent or recurrent deficiency or absence of sexual fantasies and thoughts with no desire for sex (or receptivity to sexual advances or activity). It is important to note that loss of sexual desire refers to individuals who have enjoyed sex in the past but are no longer interested.

This problem can occur because of poor physical sensations; if a person is unable to become aroused, their interest in sex is likely to diminish. It can also be due to psychological problems. But, more usually, loss of sexual interest is related to relationship or partner issues.

AROUSAL DISORDER

This problem is defined as a regular inability to attain or maintain sexual excitement. Arousal disorder tends to be a term used for women; in men this problem would be classified as erectile dysfunction (see below). However, since physical arousal is less 'obvious' in a female than a male, it can be more difficult to identify.

Physical signs of arousal in women can include: flushing of the skin, increased genital and breast sensitivity, hardening of the nipples, swelling of the clitoris, wetness or lubrication, a sense of warmth in the genitals. Poor arousal can occur at a physical level due to insufficient blood flow or nerve supply to the genital areas. A lack of sexual arousal can sometimes be due to psychological factors. However, relationship issues more frequently underlie problems of arousal.

ERECTILE DYSFUNCTION

This problem is sometimes called impotence and refers to an inability to get or keep an erection firm enough to enjoy sexual activity.

Most men are likely to experience occasional erection failure at some time in their lives, often due to psychological or relationship problems. However, if this is a persistent problem, it could be because there is a physical or medical condition that is preventing sufficient blood flows to the penis to make it hard, or because the blood drains away from the penis too quickly to keep it hard. A good indicator of a physical or medical problem is a lack of morning or nocturnal erections.

PREMATURE EJACULATION

The clinical definition of premature ejaculation is when a man ejaculates either prior to insertion of the penis, on entry, after a few thrusts, or so quickly that it becomes an issue that upsets them and/or their partners. An occasional experience of premature ejaculation is not uncommon. Most men will experience premature ejaculation at some time in their lives, which is often related to overexcitement, particularly after long periods of sexual inactivity.

It is generally believed that ejaculating too quickly is mainly due to an inability to identify the 'point of inevitability'. The physical response mechanism that enables a man to ejaculate occurs in two stages. The first stage (emission) is where the fluid enters a point at the base of the penis. When this occurs, the second stage (ejaculation – when the fluid leaves the body via the penis) is beyond the man's control and 'inevitable'.

DELAYED OR INHIBITED EJACULATION

This condition refers to when a man is unable to ejaculate, or if it takes too long to ejaculate to achieve satisfaction, which causes distress to him or his partner.

As with many other sexual problems, an inability to ejaculate could be due to a physical or medical condition that is interfering with ejaculatory reflexes. In some cases it can be due to psychological or relationship difficulties. For some men the time it takes to ejaculate will increase with age and/or duration of relationship. This can be because of greater experience and improved techniques or as a normal consequence of the ageing process, when everything tends to slow down.

However, there is also a condition referred to as retrograde ejaculation, which appears the same as delayed ejaculation but occurs because of a physical problem. When a man with this condition ejaculates, the bladder opening fails to close and all or a large proportion of the ejaculate leaks back into the bladder. If you are having a problem ejaculating and your urine appears cloudy, you should consult your doctor.

ORGASMIC DYSFUNCTION

Not being able to achieve an orgasm every time you try, or not being able to achieve one when engaging in a particular activity like intercourse or masturbation, would not be considered a sexual dysfunction. Orgasmic dysfunction refers to either a complete inability to achieve an orgasm or a markedly diminished intensity of orgasmic sensation, which causes distress.

Although it is possible, it is quite rare for men to experience ejaculation without orgasm or orgasm without ejaculation. This means that orgasmic problems in men are often dealt with as an ejaculatory disorder (see premature and delayed ejaculation above).

In women, the absence of orgasms during intercourse is not generally considered to be a sexual dysfunction. This is mainly due to the fact that many women are unable to experience an orgasm during intercourse without manual stimulation (using the hand or a vibrator).

Identifying the cause of orgasmic dysfunction is not easy, since an orgasm is a complex response that involves a combination of both subjective experience and physical changes. Physical changes can include: increased heart rate and blood pressure, rapid breathing, changes in colour of the genitals, muscle contractions and a release of physical tension. The subjective experience involves cognitive processes (that is, what we think about sex and how we perceive pleasure) and emotions (feelings of elation, intimacy, love and contentment, etc.).

Although both women and men are susceptible to the same types of physical, psychological and emotional influences, women are more likely than men to report orgasmic difficulties. It has been suggested this could be due to the hidden nature of female sex organs, which results in some women (particularly sexually inexperienced women) lacking familiarity with their own genitals and/or understanding of their sexual responses. If a woman doesn't know how to stimulate herself to orgasm, it is unlikely her partner will know.

VAGINISMUS

This problem is defined by an involuntary muscle spasm that prevents a woman from being able to have penetrative sex, insert a finger or tampon into her vagina or even have an internal examination. The muscle spasm is an automatic involuntary response similar to blinking when something is coming towards your eye.

Vaginismus is usually considered to be a fear response that might occur because of anticipated pain, fear of pregnancy, past traumatic events (for example, rape or abuse), generalised fear of intimacy or of losing control, or feelings of guilt (particularly for women with strong religious beliefs). However, given that muscle spasms are a normal response to sexual activity, it is possible that, like premature ejaculation in men, some women could experience vaginismus as a result of overexcitement, particularly on their first sexual encounter or after long periods of sexual inactivity.

DYSPAREUNIA

This is the medical term for painful sex, which is defined as recurrent or persistent genital pain associated with sexual intercourse. In women the pain can be around the vulva and/or deep inside the vagina, whereas in men it might be located in the penis shaft or tip, the scrotum or anus. Pain can be experienced before intercourse (in women during stimulation, in men when they get an erection), during penetration, orgasm/ejaculation, or after intercourse as blood flows away from the genitals.

A frequent cause of painful sex is poor lubrication; dryness in the vagina can create friction that can result in soreness of both the vagina and penis. Sex can also be painful for those with a skin condition that affects their whole body (including genitals), those with recurrent Candida (thrush), and also for some people with reduced mobility.

PEYRONIE'S DISEASE

This condition is characterised by the formation of plaque or fibrous tissue on the penis, which may be associated with curvature of the penis, erectile dysfunction and pain on erection. It tends to be more prevalent in men over 40 years of age.

Important

 For many reasons, people (particularly men) often wait up to two years before they consult a doctor (or tell their partners) about sexual problems. As some of these problems have been associated with cardiovascular disease, it is important not to wait until your MOT has run out. If you are having difficulties and they haven't passed after a few weeks of really trying, book in for a service – it could save your life.

From the Therapist's Chair

 Since the advent of oral medication such as Viagra, Cialis, Levitra and Uprima, more and more men and women believe that there is a magic pill, potion, lotion, mechanical device or medical solution to their sexual problems.

While many of these interventions are effective, they can't solve relationship problems or improve sexual technique. For example, oral treatments for erectile dysfunction are all highly effective in helping men to get an erection. However, they won't help a man to overcome feelings of inadequacy, restore his self-esteem or sexual confidence. Likewise, though it has been reported that hormone treatments have helped some men and women restore their libido, they can't solve emotional or relationship problems.

Although medical interventions can assist in restoring physical function, research has found that the success rate of medications is much higher when used in conjunction with sex therapy techniques.

Points to ponder

- Consult your doctor if you have any doubts about your health.

- Don't stop taking prescribed medication without consulting your doctor.

- Some sexual problems can be an indication of other health conditions.

- Don't be embarrassed to tell your doctor about your sexual problems.

- Medical and/or physical solutions alone won't necessarily restore your sex life.

Session 8
Sexual self

People generally understand the 'mechanics' of sex (what to do with a penis and vagina). It is only when individuals and couples encounter a problem that they might think about the other processes involved.

Sexual response involves a complex interaction of body, mind and emotions. It is important to understand how these interactions operate in order to avoid and overcome sexual difficulties. In addition, even though I agree with the principle 'If it ain't broke, don't mess with it', a little sexual knowledge can make a good thing even better.

A fundamental principle upon which sex therapy is based is that sexual response is natural: unless there are any physical, psychological or relational issues that block these responses, sexual arousal will occur. This precept led to the development of a short-term behavioural approach, which has often proved more successful than other forms of therapy. This approach uses physical exercises designed to increase knowledge and understanding of the way both our minds and bodies respond to sex.

For people to explore and understand their own responses, it is important that they do so without any pressure to 'perform' or please a partner. For this reason, sex therapy techniques usually start with information and exercises to be used by individuals, not couples. These exercises enable people to identify and overcome negative or hypercritical attitudes towards their own bodies, as well as to be aware of their own and their partner's needs. Having achieved greater awareness, they are better able to respond more fully to their partner and communicate their sexual preferences.

This session starts with a brief description of sexual responses before moving on to the practical exercises, which will help you build up your sexual confidence and improve your sexual enjoyment.

Understanding sexual responses

Sexologists use a model that distinguishes four separate aspects of sexual response: desire (wanting sex), arousal (physical sexual response), climax (achieving sexual orgasm) and resolution (when the body returns to a relaxed state). The model is based largely on physical reactions and is used to identify problems that are likely to occur in the different phases in order to consider appropriate treatments. However, since humans are thinking, feeling creatures, our sexual behaviours are far more complex than can be illustrated by a model of merely physical responses.

Whatever the reasons people engage in sex (recreation and/or procreation), their responses are based on how and what they think and feel about sex, which is often where the problems occur. In the following diagram I have combined the physical elements of the four-phase model with cognitive (thinking) and emotional (feeling) components. The descriptions of each part of the diagram will help you consider how your thoughts, emotions or physical reactions could be interfering with your sexual satisfaction, before you move on to the practical exercises.

Note: Sexual response does not necessarily follow a sequential pattern. Two-way arrows have been used in the diagram to indicate how some of the elements interact and influence each other.

Sexual response model

STIMULUS

This is the starting point when sexual thoughts and feelings can be initiated from either external or self-induced stimuli. For example, we might desire sex because we:

- see, hear, smell, taste or touch something that is sexually stimulating;

- receive some physical contact such as being kissed, hugged or caressed;

- fantasise or daydream about sex.

COGNITIVE PROCESSES (DESIRE)

This stage is usually defined as the desire to engage in sexual activity. However, simply having a desire doesn't necessarily predict how we are likely to behave. When we receive sexual stimuli, we engage in a complex cognitive process to decide if what we have experienced is sexual desire and if it is the right time, place and person.

Our decisions to act on our desire can be reinforced or inhibited by physical, emotional and behavioural responses. For example, it doesn't matter how willing the mind is – sexual desire will soon disappear if you don't have a physical response. Negative emotions can exert a similar effect. A recent argument or something that has upset you from a previous occasion can kill the most passionate of desires.

It's also worth noting that it is possible to have a physical or emotional reaction without being aware of our thoughts. As an example, I have worked with women who wanted sex but when their partners approached them they froze and panicked without knowing why.

PHYSICAL RESPONSE (AROUSAL)

This stage refers to the body preparing itself for sexual activity, such as increased genital and breast sensitivity, swelling and erection of the penis and clitoris.

Although sexual thoughts usually precede physical arousal, it is also possible for physical arousal to initiate sexual thoughts. This might happen when wearing a tight pair of jeans, riding a horse or bicycle, or waking up with an erection.

EMOTIONAL RESPONSE (AROUSAL)

Physical arousal may occur with or without sexual thoughts. But sexologists are well aware that feelings (of love or hate) towards a partner and moods (good or bad) can influence our sexual behaviour.

For some people the key to physical response is in their emotional state. For example, although we might not be thinking about sex or feeling aroused, if our partner makes us feel loved or wanted, we can become responsive to sexual advances.

BEHAVIOURAL RESPONSE (CLIMAX)

Since people engage in sexual activity that may, or may not, include climax or orgasm, this stage represents whatever sexual activity occurs.

Even though sexual thoughts and desire usually pave the way for physical and emotional responses, this is not always the case. Some people only become physically and/or emotionally aroused after they engage in sexual behaviour.

SECONDARY EMOTIONAL RESPONSE (RESOLUTION)

From a physical perspective, this phase is defined as the body returning to a 'normal' or relaxed physical state. However, after sex we experience emotions that will influence the way we think about sex. Positive feelings (of being loved or wanted) or negative feelings (of being used or abused) are remembered and will affect future sexual behaviour and pleasure.

MIND/BODY INTERACTIONS

Having considered the interactions between the mind and body, it is now time to explore your own sexual responses. The following exercises will help you overcome sexual problems by gaining a more positive view of yourself and developing your sexual confidence. As you go through each of the exercises, try to be aware of the following responses.

- **Your cognitive responses** – What are you thinking as you touch each part of your body? If you experience negative thoughts, ask yourself where they have come from and if they are realistic. For example, some people feel too embarrassed or ashamed to touch their genitals because they are brought up to believe that these are 'dirty'.

- **Your physical responses** – How does each part of your body react to your touch? If you find that you are not getting the response you expect or want, is it because you have negative thoughts about that part of your body or because you just need to change your technique?

- **Your emotional responses** – What are your feelings as you touch each part of your body? If you experience negative emotions, try to identify what they are (for example, upset, frightened) and what thoughts might be initiating these emotions.

- **Your behavioural responses** – What did you do? Did you continue to touch your body, stop at the first touch or avoid touching a specific area? If you avoided an area or quickly stopped, was it because you were uncomfortable or upset?

- **Your secondary emotions** – How did you feel after the experience? For instance, did you feel happy, contented, embarrassed, ashamed, etc.? Again check out what thoughts might have prompted these emotions.

Exercise 1 – Knowing your body

Although we might accept that there is no such thing as a perfect body (except maybe those of babies), most of us judge our own bodies quite harshly – we tend to focus on the droopy, lumpy or wrinkly bits. Real and imagined physical imperfections can make people feel less attractive and reduce their sexual confidence. But there is no need to run off to the diet club, gym or plastic surgeon. Sexual confidence does not rely on physical perfection; if it did, the world would only be populated with beautiful people. By becoming more familiar with your own body you can develop an appreciation of your sensual and sexual self, which can improve your self-image and restore your sexual confidence.

This exercise will enable you to become more familiar with your body and the way it responds to touch. The first time you do this exercise you might feel a little self-conscious, which is likely to reduce your physical reaction. But if you persevere and repeat the exercise, you will soon become comfortable and more aware of what your body enjoys.

Materials required

- Body oil or lotion

Instructions

Allow yourself about 45 minutes alone in a warm room with subdued lighting and some relaxing music. It is important not to rush this exercise; try to spend an equal amount of time on each step.

1. Remove all your clothes and lie down, using some cushions or pillows so you are supported comfortably.

2. Spend a little time relaxing. Close your eyes and take deep breaths in and out while tensing and relaxing the muscles in your arms, chest, stomach, buttocks and legs.

3. Put some body oil or lotion on your hands and, using the tips of your fingers, stroke each part of your body very slowly.

4. Start with your face, neck and shoulders; move on to your arms and hands.

5. Stroke your feet and up your legs (stroking the inside and backs of your thighs and calves), finishing with whatever you can reach of your buttocks and back.

6. Run your fingers over your chest or breasts and down to your hips, stomach and pubic areas; let your fingers run through your pubic hair but **do not** at this stage touch your vagina or penis.

7. Start to explore the sensations you like best. Use the whole of your hand and try different movements, speeds and pressures.

8. When you have finished this exercise, make yourself comfortable, relax and think about what you have learned.

   • Which parts of your body do you enjoy touching most/least?

   • Do you believe that your thoughts and/or emotions made the experiences better or worse?

   • What kind of touching does your body respond to most – light or firm, slow or fast, stroking or rubbing?

   • Were there any changes in body temperature (under your breasts, arms and between your thighs and buttocks, for instance) or in texture (tightening of your stomach muscles, hardening of nipples)?

Exercise 2 – Knowing your genitals

Although most men have more than a passing relationship with their penises, the same cannot be said for women and their vaginas. For many women and some men, touching their own genitals in a sexual way is taboo. For others genital touching is only associated with penetrative sex and orgasm. For these reasons, some people are unaware of the more subtle sensations and the full extent of their genital responses. Now that you have identified how your body responds to touch and what you enjoy, the next step is to become really familiar with your genitals.

The following exercises have been designed to ensure that you are completely familiar with your own genitals and the types of touch that produce the best response before engaging in sexual activities with your partner. When you know what pleases and arouses you, you will be able to fully respond to a partner's touch and have the confidence to tell them what you enjoy.

Before you start

Make sure you have some lubricant handy. Both male and female genitals have lots of nerve endings, which make them very sensitive, and touching them when they are dry can become uncomfortable and reduce sensuality. Since some body lotions and oil can irritate the sensitive areas around the genitals, a product specifically designed for genital lubrication (such as a water-based lubricant like KY jelly or a silicone lubricant) is best.

Allow yourself about 45 minutes alone in a warm room with subdued lighting and some relaxing music. It is important not to rush this exercise. To help you relax you might like to repeat the touching exercises in 'Knowing your body'.

Materials required

- Hand mirror or small mirror on a stand

- Lubricant

Instructions for women

1. Remove your clothes and lie down, using some cushions or pillows so you are supported comfortably.

2. Lean back, with your knees bent and legs open, and position the mirror so that you can see your genitals.

3. Using your fingers, open the outer lips (these are called the labia and are usually covered with pubic hair for protection) to expose the inner lips.

   - No two women are alike, and female genitals are rarely symmetrical. In some women the inner lips can be prominent and these may hang down between the outer lips. The colour of the lips also varies.

4. Now pull your lips open to expose your vagina, clitoris and urethra.

   - The vagina is the opening in the centre of the lips.

   - The clitoris is a small button-like protuberance (a bit like a mini penis but much more sensitive) located under the clitoral hood, which is where the inner lips meet at the top. When you are aroused, your clitoris will become erect and may be withdrawn under the clitoral hood.

   - The urethra is the small opening between the vagina and the clitoris.

5. Gently run one finger around and across your outer and inner lips and clitoris; note the difference in texture, temperature and sensation.

   - If the area is dry, using a lubricant will increase pleasurable sensations and avoid irritation.

6. When you feel ready, let your fingers slip into your vagina. Feel the texture on the inner walls and note how the texture changes as you feel further inside.

   - The vagina is usually moist, but occasionally dryness can occur, in which case you should apply more lubricant.

   - If you become aroused during this part of the exercise, notice how your clitoris becomes hard and erect, the changes in colour of your labia and the amount of moisture in your vagina.

7. Stroke the perineum (area between the vagina and anus).

8. Start to explore the sensations you like best. Vary the pressure, speed and type of touch.

   - Although this task is not intended to produce arousal or an orgasm, if it does, don't worry. Enjoy the sensation and use the opportunity to notice how your genitals respond.

   - If you begin to feel uncomfortable, stay with it for a little while. Try to find out why that particular response has come about. Be aware of your thoughts and emotions.

9. When you have finished this exercise, make yourself comfortable, relax and think about what you have learned.

   - Do you believe that your thoughts and/or emotions made the experiences better or worse?

   - What changes did you notice?

   - What did you like?

Instructions for men

1. Remove your clothes and lie down, using some cushions or pillows so you are supported comfortably.

2. Lean back, with your legs straight and slightly open, and hold the mirror so that you can see your penis.

3. Look at the top of your penis, then lift it up and look at the underside and your testes.

   • No two men are alike and male genitals are rarely symmetrical. In most men one testicle can be slightly larger than the other, and one testicle (usually the left) hangs slightly lower than the other.

4. Run your fingers around the glans (the head or tip of your penis) and the frenulum (the smooth area below the glans), then up and down the shaft of your penis.

   • If your penis is soft, notice its weight and texture in your hand.

5. Stroke your scrotum, gently massaging each testicle.

6. Lift your scrotum and stroke your perineum (area between the testicles and anus).

7. Start to explore the sensations you like best.

   • If you are uncircumcised, try drawing back your foreskin very slightly, and then pull it up again to cover your glans.

   • If you are circumcised, move the skin covering your penis, squeezing and releasing it to produce sensations in your glans.

8. Vary the pressure, speed and type of touch.

   • Although this task is not intended to produce an erection or orgasm, if it does, don't worry. Enjoy the sensation and use the opportunity to notice how your genitals respond.

   • If you begin to feel uncomfortable, stay with it for a little while. Try to find out why that particular response has come about. Be aware of your thoughts and emotions.

9. When you have finished this exercise, make yourself comfortable and relax. Think about what you have learned.

   • Do you believe that your thoughts and/or emotions made the experiences better or worse?

   • What changes did you notice?

   • What did you like?

 ## Exercise 3 – Toning up

Kegel exercises (sometimes called pelvic floor exercises) are frequently recommended by sex therapists since they tighten vaginal muscles, strengthen the muscles surrounding the penis and improve blood supply to the genitals. Doing the exercises can increase sensitivity, enhance awareness of sexual sensations and improve sexual response and orgasmic sensations.

This exercise is about toning up the pelvic floor muscles. Before you start, you need to identify your pelvic floor muscles, which comprise a hammock of muscles supporting the bowel and bladder in the abdomen. There are two simple methods that will help you recognise these muscles. The first is to stop yourself from passing wind from your bowels by clenching your anus. The second is to try to stop the flow when you are urinating.

Since no one else will be aware that you are doing Kegel exercises, you can do them anywhere and at any time.

Instructions

1. Stand, sit or lie with your knees slightly apart (no need to get undressed for this one).

2. Slowly squeeze and release your pelvic floor muscles 15 times; try to hold each contraction (or squeeze) for five seconds.

3. Repeat the exercise, but instead of holding the contraction for five seconds, let go immediately so that you can feel a quick lift in your pelvic floor.

4. Once you have mastered the technique, try combining the fast and slow exercises.

5. Repeat 15 sets of slow and 15 sets of fast as many times in the day as you can. Remember, no one can see you doing these exercises so you can do them anywhere and any time.

As with all exercises, the more effort you put in, the better and quicker the results.

Note: Kegel exercises are particularly good for increasing the time it takes to orgasm or ejaculate. A technique for controlling ejaculation and orgasms during intercourse using Kegel exercises is included in Session 9, 'Getting it together'.

Exercise 4 – Body mapping

The final step in your individual programme is to tell your partner what you have discovered. Although your body might now be very familiar territory to you, to your partner it could still be a strange and wondrous land. But it is not so easy to describe the 'landscape' of your body in words, which means you need to show them the parts of your body you like being touched. One way to do this would be to undress and show them what you have learned. However, this is not recommended, since it could lead to sexual excitement (for one or both of you), which is likely to disengage the brain and prevent discussion. Therefore, this exercise involves drawing a 'body map' to help you explain exactly which parts of your body you like being touched and what you want to change.

Materials required

- Paper

- Different coloured felt-tipped pens or pencils

Instructions

1. Draw an outline of a body on both sides of a sheet of paper, one to represent the front of your body and one, the back.

   - It doesn't need to be a work of art – just recognisable as a body with head, arms and legs.

2. Draw a picture of your genitals on a separate sheet of paper. But don't worry if you are not an artist.

   - For men, a rectangle shape with a circle at one end to represent the head of your penis and two circles at the other for your testicles will be sufficient.

   - For women, all you need are three oval shapes inside each other to represent your outer and inner lips and vagina with a small dot or circle at the top to represent your clitoris.

3. Using different-coloured pens, mark on your drawings which parts of your body and genitals you:

   - dislike being touched;

   - like being touched;

   - find sensual.

4. Explain to your partner:

    - why you do not like to be touched on areas you dislike;

    - how you like to be touched on areas you like;

    - how you like to be touched on the sensual areas.

From the Therapist's Chair

For many of the people I see in therapy, it is not simply a lack of knowledge about their own bodies that prevents them from enjoying a full sex life, but their inhibitions. The thoughts and feelings they have about sex often make it difficult for them to be responsive to their own sexual needs and/or their partner's advances.

Many of the 'hang-ups' we have about sex arise because of attitudes and beliefs people have about what they ought, or ought not, to feel or do. Some people experience guilt about enjoying sex and find it difficult to give themselves 'permission' to try new sensations or experiences. Others find it difficult to accept their own sexual feelings and mentally detach themselves when making love, becoming a 'spectator' instead of a participant. For some, fear or embarrassment about what might happen if they lose control is an issue.

Before an individual can become a good lover, they need to know and understand their own bodies. Exploring your own thoughts and emotions will help you identify and overcome attitudes and beliefs that are limiting your sexual enjoyment. Learning about your body and sexual responses will ensure you know what your body needs to achieve sexual satisfaction and enable you to tell your partner what you would like them to do.

Points to ponder

- If you don't know how to sexually satisfy your own needs, your partner doesn't stand much of a chance.

- Don't let unhelpful thoughts and emotions about sex spoil your sexual enjoyment.

- Give yourself permission to enjoy sex and try new experiences.

Session 9
Getting it together

One of the most frequent comments I hear from the people I see in sex therapy is: 'I want it to be like it used to be.' I usually point out that I am not a Time Lord and, even if I were, *they* are not like they used to be, so turning back the clock won't work. Besides, 'what it used to be like' isn't always as good as we remember and may not be right for where we are at now. At this stage in therapy, I encourage couples to undertake a series of homework exercises that will allow them to understand and adapt to their physical, emotional and sexual changes. Instead of turning back the clock, they 'start afresh' and explore techniques that can improve their sexual responses, increase pleasure and help them rediscover the passions they long for.

In this session you will be building on what you discovered about your own body in Session 8, 'Sexual self'. By using the techniques you have learned, you and your partner will be able to practise mutual sensual touch and exploration of each other's bodies before moving on to penetrative sex.

Sensuality

The focus in the next two exercises is on the sensations you perceive while touching and being touched, without the demands of performance or an ultimate goal of orgasm or penetrative sex. These exercises are particularly helpful for people who have difficulty in relaxing and enjoying sex because of fears about sexual performance. Since your only goal in these first exercises is to enjoy the experience and not to 'perform', you cannot fail.

Removing performance expectations will enable you to learn to:

- trust your partner to touch you in a way that is enjoyable;

- ask your partner to 'stop' without fear of upsetting them;

- discover or rediscover the pleasures of tender, sensual and imaginative intimacy;

- explore your sexual thoughts and emotional responses.

Before you start, I have listed below some questions frequently asked by couples in therapy about the exercises.

Do I/we have to be naked to do the exercises?

The exercises are more effective if you are both completely naked. If you have particular difficulty in being naked with your partner, you can start the first exercise with as few clothes as you feel comfortable in and aim to reduce the number of items you are wearing each time you do the exercise.

How often should we do each exercise?

In face-to-face therapy, the number of times each homework exercise is undertaken depends on the difficulties a couple has been experiencing. In DIY therapy, you and your partner are going to be the judges of what you need and what is right for you. As a general guide, to benefit from these exercises you should undertake each one as many times as necessary for you both to feel comfortable before moving on to the next exercise.

Why do we have to spend time on all of each other's bodies rather than on one particular area?

During penetrative sexual activity, people often ignore large areas of the body that are full of responsive nerves. By touching all of the body you will be able to discover new feelings and sensations and identify likes and dislikes that can later be included (or avoided) during lovemaking.

What if I don't experience sexual feelings during the exercises?

Many people find these exercises strange at first, which may make them a bit tense and unable to connect their partner's touch with sexual feelings. Just keep in mind that the idea is simply to relax and enjoy whatever sensations you are experiencing.

What if one or both of us become sexually aroused?

The aim of the first three exercises is to reduce performance anxiety and help you recognise that you can enjoy the feelings of arousal without it leading to orgasm or penetrative sex. If you find you become very aroused, you may want to relieve this by masturbating. But it is important that you do so in private. If you try to involve your partner, you might make them feel pressured to engage in further sexual activity before they are ready.

What if one or both of us wants to go on and have penetrative sex?

It is very important that you agree **not** to have penetrative sex until you have completed the first two exercises and both feel you are ready. Remember, the aim of these exercises is to help you overcome past problems, increase intimacy and gain more sensual pleasure from your relationship. If you rush, or are pressured, into penetrative sex, you are unlikely to be able to identify or resolve problems.

What if I feel anxious during an exercise?

It is not uncommon for some people to feel anxious while undertaking some of these exercises. Simply tell your partner you feel anxious and ask them to stop to allow you time to relax before they continue. If you continue to feel anxious, ask them to change what they are doing or move to a different area and try again when you next repeat the exercise.

What if I feel discomfort or pain?

Tell your partner and ask them to stop doing whatever is causing pain, and move the touching a little away from that area. It may help to touch that area yourself and see what happens. If the pain persists, you should consult your doctor.

What if distracting thoughts come into my mind?

If you find it difficult to concentrate on the experience, think about your breathing and try to focus on the sensations. Is your breathing shallow or deep? Is your skin warm or cool? Are your muscles relaxed or tense?

Exercise 1 – Sensual touch

This exercise involves you and your partner taking it in turns to touch, stroke and caress each other's bodies. As you are doing this exercise, you should remember it is not about 'performing' for your partner's pleasure. It is not a massage session, nor is it about achieving an orgasm or engaging in penetrative sex. The aim of this exercise is to promote relaxation, eliminate anxieties about sexual performance and discover new ways to be intimate together.

Before you start

You should both agree not to touch each other's nipples, breasts or genital areas. Some of you might find this difficult, but it is essential, particularly if you haven't had sex for a while, you have problems with sex or you are just not enjoying the sex. By removing the pressure to 'perform', you are better able to overcome anxieties about sex and get out of old habits by learning new ways to be intimate.

For this exercise (and Exercise 2 on page 119) you will need to set aside about an hour when you can be alone, without interruptions. Since these exercises suggest the use of body lotions, oils or sexual lubricants, make sure you have these to hand before you start. Find a room that is comfortable, warm and private, with somewhere to lie down. Prepare the room in a way that makes it inviting; for example, you could use soft lighting (a small lamp or candles) and play some soft music. Don't forget to turn off your telephone(s) and switch off computers, televisions, etc. Prepare yourselves by having a bath or shower.

Note: If your bedroom reminds you of sexual difficulties, or past failures, it is a good idea to try to find another room.

Instructions

1. Take your clothes off, lie down on the bed next to each other and spend a little time relaxing.

2. Take deep breaths in and out while tensing and relaxing the muscles in your arms, chest, stomach, buttocks and legs, finishing with a few contractions of your pelvic muscles (Kegel exercises described in Session 8, 'Sexual self').

3. Next, one of you should get comfortable lying face down, while your partner takes up a sitting or kneeling position that allows them to touch every part of the back of your body.

    • Sensual touching starts with the back because this area is not as readily associated with sexual activity and touching it usually produces a relaxed state.

4. Start by stroking your partner's toes and feet, moving slowly up their legs to the buttocks. From here, move on to the back, neck, arms and hands. Finally, stroke your partner's hair and run your fingers across their scalp. Focus on your own sensations. Think about how the different textures of your partner's body feel, and notice the part you enjoy caressing most. If your partner tells you that they do not like a particular touch and asks you to stop, you must respect their wishes.

    • You can use your fingertips, palms, back of hands, arms, lips, tongue, hair or even eyelashes. Try using a variety of touches (slow, fast, gentle, firm, licking or nibbling). You could even experiment with body lotion, oil or different fabrics (for example, silk, fur, leather, velvet or feathers). Men often prefer a firmer touch than women, but the important thing to remember is to do whatever your partner enjoys.

- When you are being touched, try not to direct your partner; instead, remain passive and receptive, enjoying the sensations. Let your partner know in words or gestures what you are feeling. Move your partner's hands to indicate the areas you most like being touched; you could place your hand over theirs to show them the type of touch and pressure you like. This will help your partner understand what pleases you and prevent you from 'spectatoring', which is when you watch your body being touched without feeling the sensations. If you feel uncomfortable, you can gently move your partner's hand or ask them to stop, but try to continue after you have had time to relax. If you are unable to continue, ask them to move to a different area and try again the next time you do the exercise.

5. After 10 minutes, ask your partner to turn over and lie on their back. Stroke and caress the front of their body (but not nipples, breasts or genital areas). Again, begin with their feet, gradually moving up to their stomach (but not genitals), chest (but not breasts), arms, hands and neck. Finish by kissing their eyes, ears and mouth (but not passionate kissing at this stage) and stroking their hair and head.

   - If one or both of you become sexually aroused during this exercise, simply enjoy the sensation of becoming aroused and then try to let it go. This action isn't designed to frustrate or annoy you but to demonstrate how female arousal and male erections can be gained and lost without it being a problem, as well as enjoyed without orgasm, ejaculation or penetrative sex. Besides, this is a good way of learning how to delay ejaculation. If you do become very aroused, you may want to relieve this by masturbating. But it is important that you do this in private; if you try to involve your partner, you might make them feel pressured to engage in sexual activity before they are ready.

6. Now it is time to change places so that your partner can stroke and caress your body in the same way.

7. When you have finished, lie in each other's arms and talk to each other about what you were thinking and feeling during the exercise. Pay equal attention to the good and easy parts, as well as any areas that did not feel so good. You might ask each other the following questions.

   - What felt good?

   - What was difficult?

   - Were you sexually aroused?

   - Was it frustrating?

- What did you learn?

- Which felt more comfortable – touching or being touched?

- Did you feel relaxed or anxious?

8. Repeat the exercise until such time that you are comfortable receiving your partner's touch, before moving on to the next exercise.

Exercise 2 – Genital touch

This exercise involves exploring the breast and genital areas, but it still does not involve penetrative sex. The aim of this exercise is not to try to arouse your partner or give them an orgasm (although this might happen). It is simply to enable you both to learn about what your partner likes, as well as to enjoy the experience of sexual touch for its own sake.

Instructions

1. Start by repeating what you did in Exercise 1 – 'Sensual touch', but focus on the areas you identified as the most enjoyable. After stroking these areas, you can begin to include breasts, nipples and genital touching.

   - When stroking breasts, nipples and genitals, you should not concentrate your efforts solely on these parts. Move from these areas to other parts of the body and back again, as naturally as possible.

2. Touching a male partner

   - Start by tracing the lines of his chest, moving slowly to his nipples; try using the type of touch you enjoy receiving. Experiment with gently touching his inner thighs and the testicles and then build up to stroking, holding or rubbing the penis shaft, frenulum (the area just underneath the head of his penis) and glans (the head of his penis). Remember that the glans is particularly sensitive to touch, so be gentle. It doesn't matter if the penis is erect or flaccid during this exercise.

   - Use different types of touch and ask him which ones he prefers. Vary the speed, direction, pressure and degree of stimulation. If he gets an erection, continue to stroke his penis for a while but move to another part of his body until the erection subsides before caressing it again. This action isn't designed to frustrate or annoy your partner but to demonstrate to both of you how an erection can be gained and lost without it being a problem, as well as enjoyed without ejaculation/orgasm or penetrative sex.

- Orgasm isn't the objective here. If your partner becomes highly aroused, he can relieve this by masturbating alone or, if you are willing, you can continue manual stimulation until he reaches a climax.

3. Touching a female partner

- Start by stroking and cupping your partner's breasts and then gently kissing, licking and sucking her nipples. Run your hands across her belly and genital areas. Run your fingers through her pubic hair and then down the tops of her thighs very slowly to her inner thighs. Bring your hand up to cup her pubic areas and gently run your fingers down between her legs to stroke the outer lips of her vagina. Using a sexual lubricant, gently part the outer lips to expose the clitoris. Softly stroke the entrance to the vagina and clitoris (do not rub hard or use direct pressure but stroke it softly and lightly). If she is willing, but only if she is willing, you can go on to slowly and gently put one or more fingers into her vagina.

- Use different types of touch and ask her which ones she prefers. Vary the speed, direction, pressure and degree of stimulation. Experiment with stopping and starting from time to time. This can demonstrate how arousal can be achieved and enjoyed without orgasm or penetrative sex.

- Orgasm isn't the objective here. If your partner becomes highly aroused, she can relieve this by masturbating alone or, if you are willing, you can continue manual stimulation until she reaches a climax.

4. When you have finished, lie in each other's arms and talk to each other about what you were thinking and feeling during the exercise. Pay equal attention to the good and easy parts, as well as any areas that did not feel so good. You might ask each other the following questions.

- What felt good?

- What was difficult?

- Which felt more comfortable – touching or being touched?

- Did you feel relaxed or anxious?

5. Repeat the exercise until such time that you are comfortable receiving your partner's touch, before moving on to the next exercise.

Exercise 3 – Holding on

By the time couples get to this exercise, they are usually eager for penetrative sex. However, you should beware of falling back into old habits. No matter how eager or sexually frustrated you might feel, try to remember that doing it slowly prolongs your pleasure.

This exercise is designed to help both of you enjoy the experience of penetration in a new way. If either one or both of you want to go on to climax, during or after this exercise, that's okay – but not a requirement to enjoy the experience.

Instructions

1. Set the scene as you have done previously and spend some time enjoying each other's bodies, drawing on everything you have already practised. But remember:

    -   Women need to be adequately aroused and relaxed before penetration begins. Men often assume women are ready long before they actually are, so it is important that she tells you when she is ready for penetration.

    -   Similarly, men will need an adequate erection for penetration – but this does not mean their penis has to be extremely hard. If you use a lubricant, you should be able to achieve penetration with a less erect penis than you might have previously thought was necessary.

2. Put plenty of lubricant on the penis and at the entrance to the vagina. Relax and breathe slowly, and then move into either the woman-on-top, side-by-side or scissors position. These positions are recommended since, unlike man-on-top, they allow easier access to a woman's clitoris (by either the woman or her partner), they allow women to have more control over depth of penetration and enable men to relax.

    -   *Woman-on-top* is ideal for most sexual problems. In this position, the woman kneels astride her partner, facing him with her legs either side of his body and sitting gently on his upper thighs.

    -   *Side-by-side* is a very relaxing position – and good if you are tired or if you have problems with your joints and kneeling is difficult. In this position you lie side-by-side, facing each other, and the woman puts her legs around her partner's waist.

- *Scissors position* involves a man lying on his side while his partner lies on her back at an angle of approximately 45 degrees with her legs over the man's hips so that her calves are resting on his bottom (making a shape similar to a small letter 't'). The entrance to her vagina should be snug against her partner's pelvis.

3. Gently and slowly guide the penis into the vagina and when it is inside as far as is comfortable for both of you, stop and breathe deeply. Do not move – just hold the position for as long as possible and enjoy the sensations and feelings it creates.

    - If the man begins to lose his erection, the woman can try flexing her vagina muscles and ask him to flex his penis (Kegel exercises).

4. When you have held this position for as long as you can, the man should remove his penis and you should lie in each other's arms and relax.

5. Repeat the exercise as many times as you wish, but with each repetition try to increase the time you spend in this 'holding' exercise.

Exercise 4 – Slow and sensual

Couples often think of penetrative sex in terms of vigorous thrusting, which can feel good, but this type of movement can mask more subtle sensations that could increase pleasure. With less movement and exertion, you can bring the elusive sensations in your genitals fully into conscious awareness. This exercise will help you explore some slow, sensual techniques that can enhance your sexual experiences.

Instructions

1. Set the scene as you have done previously, and spend some time enjoying each other's bodies, drawing on everything you have already practised.

2. Start by following the instructions for Exercise 3 – 'Holding on' (above), but this time the man should begin to move his penis very slowly and gently while he or his partner stimulates her clitoris.

    - Make it slow and sensuous, so that each of you really has time to enjoy every sensation. Make eye contact, telling each other your feelings and what you are experiencing while stroking each other's bodies.

    - Do not worry about the firmness of the man's erection, but instead relax and enjoy each other's attention. If the penis slips out of the vagina at any time, don't worry – just slip it gently back in. If it is not hard enough to penetrate again, either of you might like to spend some time stimulating the penis before trying again.

3. Continue with the movements, varying the pace and stopping and restarting to heighten the sensations.

- If either of you wants to go on to climax, that's okay – but it is certainly not a requirement. If you do not climax, this does not mean that the exercise has been a waste of time. Try to remember that only practice makes perfect.

Exercise 5 – Prolonging enjoyment

Sexual enjoyment isn't simply about how long sex lasts because, forgive the pun, there aren't any hard and fast rules. Satisfaction can be had from an occasional 'quickie', especially in the morning just before you leave for work, or a marathon that lasts for days – eating breakfast, lunch and dinner off each other's bodies. What is important is that sex should last at least as long as you and your partner want and need.

In Session 8, 'Sexual self', you were introduced to the Kegel exercises to help you improve your own sexual responses and sensations and prepare you for sex. However, Kegel exercises can also be used during sexual intercourse to help extend your enjoyment. By using a combination of Kegel and breathing techniques, ejaculation can be delayed and orgasms enhanced. For this reason, therapists often recommend them for people with sexual problems (particularly for arousal and orgasmic difficulties and premature ejaculation).

If you are experiencing ejaculation or orgasmic problems, or if you just want to experiment with how long you can last, you might want to try the following exercise.

Instructions

1. During penetrative sex breathe deeply, avoiding rapid shallow breathing (breathing abdominally helps you to be aware of your internal sexual organs).

- Use only the necessary muscles to perform the pelvic movement and use a minimum of muscular tension – in particular, avoid using the buttocks when thrusting forward.

2. Combine abdominal breathing with the pelvic movement: inhale when drawing the pelvis back and exhale when moving the pelvis forward.

- The penis reacts much more to friction than to pressure, whereas the opposite is true for the vagina. Consequently, a slow forward or backward tilting pelvic motion by the woman will increase her sexual stimulation by augmenting the pressure against the vaginal wall without providing much friction to her partner's penis.

3. Vary the speed, intensity and amount of pelvic movement.

4. As you are approaching ejaculation/orgasm, try to identify the muscles in the pelvis (this helps delay the response). Stop moving, relax every muscle and breathe abdominally; avoid trying to hold back the ejaculation/orgasm by contracting muscles.

5. Breathe with the mouth open and jaw relaxed; this makes it possible to exhale faster, reduce pressure in the ribcage and decrease muscular tension.

6. Spread legs apart. Sexual excitement tends to bring the legs together, whereas reversing this reaction helps to delay ejaculation/orgasm.

7. Change positions, experiment with various positions and analyse the effects that they produce on levels of muscular tension, breathing and ability to perform the pelvic movement.

Techniques to help with specific problems

The exercises in this session can be used not only to make good sex even better, but also in the treatment of specific sexual problems. Below are some additional tips and techniques that you might find useful if you are experiencing a particular problem.

Fantasy

Loss of sexual desire is specifically associated with a lack of sexual thoughts or fantasies. However, intrusive thoughts can also impede arousal and the ability to achieve orgasm. If your mind wanders when you are being sexual (on to things like work or what you forgot to get from the shops) you are likely to 'go off the boil'. Sexual fantasy can help regain desire, keep you focused and block out intrusive thoughts (see Session 10, 'Fun and fantasy').

Lubricants

These are recommended to make the sensation of touch feel softer and more sensuous, especially in areas which have a lot of nerve endings, such as the clitoris, penis and scrotum. Though there are a number of lubricants available, silicone-based lubricants tend to be better than oil- or water-based lubricants: they are safe to use with condoms and birth control methods, do not stain or cause irritation, and they are waterproof and long-lasting. There are some lubricants containing an amino acid called l'arginine that can enhance arousal by stimulating blood flow and make the area become warm and tingle. But a word of warning – some of these should not be used with sex toys.

Vibrators

Some men and women need additional stimulation to achieve or maintain arousal and/ or orgasm. There is a wide variety of vibrating devices that can be used by both men and women to stimulate genital response. Larger vibrators can be used on the penis, scrotum, vagina and anus. There are also small, battery-operated vibrators designed to stimulate the clitoris. In addition, there are vacuum vibrating devices that are applied to the clitoris (similar to vacuum pumps for men, but much smaller). These are designed to increase blood flow to the genitals to increase sensation and improve arousal and vaginal lubrication. One that has been approved by the US Food and Drug Administration for female arousal disorders is called Eros.

Masturbation techniques

Self-stimulation or masturbatory techniques are often recommended by sex therapists for men with premature ejaculation to learn how to recognise and control different levels of arousal. There are two variations, both of which involve stimulating the penis until the man is on the verge of ejaculation and then stopping or squeezing the penis to prevent ejaculation. The squeeze technique involves squeezing firmly (with a thumb on the frenulum, and the two fingers on the opposite side of the penis where the glans meets the shaft) for a few seconds. Both stop–start and squeeze techniques have to be repeated until a man can recognise when ejaculation is likely to occur.

Vacuum pumps and rings

These devices are generally used to help men to achieve and/or maintain an erection. In addition, since they stimulate blood flow, they are useful as a 'penis gym' for men who have not had an erection for quite a while.

Vacuum pumps

A vacuum pump is a clear plastic tube that is placed over the penis and uses suction (via a hand- or battery-operated pump mechanism) to draw blood into the penis to create an erection. Vacuum pumps are particularly useful for those who are not able to use oral medications.

Constriction rings

These enable men to keep an erection and are usually used in conjunction with vacuum devices. However, men who are able to get a natural erection can also use them. They are expandable bands that are placed at the base of the penis to trap the blood (similar to a tourniquet). A constriction ring must be removed within 30 minutes of placing it on the penis in order to allow circulation to return to normal.

Penile scrotal rings

Like constriction rings, these are also used to help men keep their erection. Penile scrotal rings can be made of rigid silicone or chrome. They are placed over the flaccid penis and testicles, close to the body. When an erection develops, the pressure of the expanding penis against the ring traps the blood, thereby maintaining the erection. Penile scrotal rings should not be worn with an erect penis for more than 30 minutes at any one time.

Vaginal trainers

Sex therapists often recommend vaginal trainers for women with vaginismus. Vaginal trainers are usually made of smooth plastic, shaped like a phallus, and come in different sizes. They are available without prescription and usually come with detailed instructions. Briefly, women with vaginismus are encouraged to learn about and become aware of their bodies through the use of such techniques as Kegel exercises and sensual self-exploration. Then vaginal trainers are used to help them become accustomed to penetration by starting with small trainers and moving on to larger trainers before engaging in penetrative sex with their partners. However, since women with vaginismus often have emotional and/or psychological issues associated with penetration, without professional support the use of trainers might not help and could even be detrimental.

From the Therapist's Chair

When couples in therapy have successfully completed the exercises in this session, they have the techniques needed to help them overcome sexual difficulties and enhance their sexual experiences. But a satisfying sexual relationship needs more than technical expertise in the bedroom. Building or rebuilding a secure intimate relationship requires both partners to continually strive towards their mutual satisfaction and pleasure.

People often make the mistake of believing that sex is something that generally occurs at a specified time (usually at night) and in a particular place (usually the bedroom), and foreplay is only done prior to penetrative sex. These notions lead to the assumption that no matter what has happened prior to bedtime a partner can, like a light switch, be 'turned on' to sex. While this might be the case for some people, most are more like a volume knob that needs to be turned up slowly and gently throughout the day with 'foreplay'.

Foreplay should start the minute you wake up and continue until you fall asleep, regardless of whether or not you want or are planning sexual activity. I am not talking about constantly touching or groping your partner in a sexual way but about being affectionate and acknowledging your partner whenever you are together with small gestures, smiles and words. This 'affectionate foreplay' not only makes a partner feel loved, secure and wanted but it can also make them feel sexually attractive and a lot more interested in sex.

Ultimately, although sexual techniques can enhance physical enjoyment and help you overcome sexual difficulties, without affectionate foreplay you are unlikely to get the opportunity to demonstrate your technical proficiency.

Points to ponder

- Sex is not about orgasms and penetration but about enjoying the physical and emotional intimacy you share.

- Getting stuck at some point doesn't mean you have failed but that you have more time to enjoy what you are doing and explore your way forward.

- Being a sensual expert is better than trying to be a sexual technician.

- Becoming a good lover means being able to give and receive pleasure.

Session 10
Fun and fantasy

Most therapy programmes end when couples have resolved their relationship problems and/or learned some of the techniques to deal with or overcome their sexual difficulties. But I believe this is just the beginning. The euphoria experienced by the relief of overcoming a problem can lull people into a false sense of security. It is all too easy to forget about the changes they have made and return to the old habits that brought about their problems in the first place.

Ultimately, prevention has to be better than cure. In order to prevent problems occurring or recurring, it is vital to nurture what is good and joyful. For this reason, I encourage couples to explore the fun, fantasy and playfulness of sex. Some people might think this is trivial, believing that love and adequate sexual function are all that are required for relationship fulfilment. But sexual playfulness can:

- demonstrate trust and the importance placed on mutual happiness and pleasures;

- move people beyond idealised notions of romantic or erotic sex that 'must' culminate in penetration;

- aid relaxation, relieve performance anxieties, protect against disappointment and prevent sexual boredom;

- put a smile on your face.

To say that couples who play together stay together might sound a little trite – but it is none the less true. It is worth repeating here something from Session 5, 'Romance': 'Playtime isn't just for children; adult play is essential for personal health and relationship success.'

The focus of your DIY therapy is now on discovering or rediscovering the fun of sex. All you need to do is open your mind to new things and allow yourself to be a little adventurous.

Note: There are exercises in this session with activities that some might consider a bit risqué. My aim is not to offend but to provide you with some ideas that the couples I have worked with in therapy have found useful.

Sexual fantasy

Some people believe that having sexual fantasies means you don't love your partner or that you are being disloyal. But fantasies do not have to include other people or even real people; it's your imagination so it can be anything that you enjoy. Sexual fantasies can be romantic, erotic, pornographic, safe or dangerous.

There are two important things to understand about fantasies. First, they aren't real; sexual fantasies are no more real than the idle daydreams you might have about winning the lottery, becoming a world-class sports person or living for ever. Second, what you fantasise about doesn't necessarily indicate what you want to do; many people fantasise about things like group sex, bondage and sadomasochism but in reality they know these activities would be a definite 'turn-off'. Others might have fantasies about impossible or impractical scenarios like sex on a moving motorcycle or indulging in bodice-ripping period dramas.

So, what are the benefits? Well, fantasising is simply a mechanism that can help to keep you focused on your sexual pleasure, prevent your mind from wandering and block out thoughts of failure to keep you aroused and reach orgasm.

FANTASY IN ACTION

Fantasies are generally recognised as part of a healthy sexual relationship. Their sole purpose would seem to be to induce desire, arousal and pleasurable sexual feelings.

If you and your partner are comfortable sharing your personal fantasies, that's fine. If not, you could make something up based on a scenario your partner would find exciting. Some people find it difficult to talk to their partners about fantasies. If this is the case, you could start by writing them down or sharing them over the telephone.

There is a large range of adult materials, magazines, DVDs, books, etc., which have been produced to appeal to both women and men. However, you should not try to introduce erotic materials into your relationship unless you are sure your partner is likely to become aroused by them.

It may surprise you to learn that the biggest and most important sex organ you have is between your ears. With a little practice, you will probably be able to create better and more appropriate fantasies for yourself and each other than anyone else. And they are free!

 Exercise 1 – Showtime

This exercise is a frequent fantasy for many people. Nonetheless, it is by far one of the most difficult sexual exercises you will do. Without fail, when I suggest this exercise to couples in therapy, at least one of the partners looks at me in terror. But none of the couples I have worked with has ever refused, and all agree that the rewards are worth it.

In this exercise you will be masturbating in front of your partner to show them how they might bring you to orgasm. Although the exercise can aid excitement and might fulfil one of your fantasies, this is not its main aim. Its primary purpose is to help you overcome your inhibitions; a secondary purpose is to give your partner a clearer understanding of what you like.

Materials required

- Sexual lubricant

Instructions

1. Okay, you know the drill by now. A warm comfortable room, soft lights, music etc., get naked or wear something you feel sexy in.

   - You may want to set the scene as erotic or educational and have some fun as his/her teacher.

2. Sit on the bed or a chair facing your partner, who should be far enough away to see, but not touch.

3. Start touching the areas of your body that you find most enjoyable and sensual.

4. Put some sexual lubricant on your fingers, expose your genitals and start to touch them (as you did in Session 8, Exercise 2 – 'Knowing your genitals').

5. Show your partner what you like and how you achieve arousal and orgasm through self-stimulation.

   - You should try to feel as free and uninhibited as possible to enable your partner to get as clear an understanding as possible of your own personal preferences. If you find this difficult, you might like to close your eyes and focus on the sensations.

6. Continue until you reach orgasm. If you are unable to reach orgasm, don't worry, most people find this difficult the first few times; just stop when you are ready.

7. When you have finished, cover yourself up and join your partner for a cuddle.

   - This exercise can make some people feel emotionally vulnerable. Therefore, it is very important for your partner to show their appreciation of the gift you have given them with physical, not sexual, affection.

8. Talk to each other about the experience: tell your partner how you felt and feel, ask them how it made them feel and what they have learned.

9. Now it is time for your partner to show you what pleases them.

Exercise 2 – Oral sex snacks

Many people I see in therapy already enjoy oral sex as part of their sexual play. Some will never engage in this activity (and that's fine) but others, for many reasons, are reluctant to try. The main benefit of oral sex is that the moisture and softness of lips and tongue can be more stimulating than fingers or sex toys.

This exercise provides information for those who would like to try oral sex with or without a favourite appetiser.

Materials required

- Optional: any food you like that is lickable (such as yoghurt, honey, chocolate spread, etc.)

Instructions

1. Same as before. A warm comfortable room, soft lights, music, etc., get naked or wear something that makes you feel sexy.

2. Start with the sensual touch exercises (in Session 9, 'Getting it together'), focusing first on the areas you identified as most enjoyable before moving to the genitals.

   - Oral sex on a woman (cunnilingus). Gently use your fingers to open your partner's outer lips, exposing her clitoris and vagina. Use your tongue to gently lick around the clitoral area, alternating between slow and flicking movements. While doing this, you can also use your finger to tease open the entrance to her vagina. Alternatively, you could try putting your tongue inside the entrance to her vagina, while stimulating her clitoris with your finger. Experiment (you might even try sucking or blowing on her clitoris and inner lips) and let your partner tell you what she enjoys.

- Oral sex on a man (fellatio). Gently lick and kiss your partner's testicles, running your tongue up the shaft of his penis then flicking your tongue across, and rubbing your lips around, the tip/head (glans). While you are doing this, continue to stroke his testicles and perineum (area between the scrotum and anus). Be careful if you are sucking your partner's penis not to irritate it with your teeth or take his penis further into your mouth than you can manage (which might activate the 'gag' reflex). If your partner gets very excited, he might want to ejaculate. Some people are happy to let their partner ejaculate into their mouths, whereas others are not. It's a good idea to discuss your preference with your partner beforehand, so you both know where you stand.

- Simultaneous oral sex. The position referred to as the '69' will enable you both to give and receive oral stimulation at the same time. This position involves facing your partner and lying with your head near your partner's genitals while their head is near your genitals. Some couples do this with one partner lying above the other, while others find it easier if they both lie on their sides.

- Oral sex with food. Spread your favourite lickable food on your partner's chest/breast, stomach and genitals (since this can get messy you might want to lie on a towel) and lick them clean.

3. When you have finished, cuddle up and tell each other how you felt and are feeling now.

Exercise 3 – Sexercises

There are hundreds of different sexual positions: some take little effort while others require extreme flexibility and athleticism. Trying out new positions can be fun but also very frustrating if they don't work.

This exercise will help you make sure you find positions that are suitable to you both, without the pressure of performance. It also has the added advantage of providing a fun way to exercise with your partner and practise your Kegel exercises.

Before you start

List as many different sexual positions as you can both think of. These should include all the positions you can think of, such as: sitting; standing; kneeling; and lying down, side-by-side, face-to-face and face-to-back.

Instructions

1. Set aside 15 minutes in a room where you will have privacy.

2. Choose six sexual positions.

3. Get into your first sexual position.

4. Slowly squeeze and release your pelvic floor muscles (Kegel exercises):

   - 15 times, holding each contraction (or squeeze) for five seconds;

   - ten times, letting go immediately so that you can feel a quick lift in your pelvic floor.

5. Repeat the above for the remaining five sexual positions.

6. The next time you do your sexercises, choose different positions.

Exercise 4 – Sexual fun cards

The type of things couples do when they engage in sexual play depends on what they view as arousing, pleasurable and desirable. The adage 'different strokes for different folks' certainly applies to sexual behaviour. Below is a list of things most people find enjoyable:

- wearing special clothes (fancy underwear, leather, rubber, fancy dress);

- role playing (acting out sex fantasies, assuming fantasy characters);

- playing with sexual 'toys' (vibrators, dildos, sexual cards or board games);

- watching erotic movies, reading erotic stories together;

- using special places (hotels, beach, woods, office, car);

- teasing (romantic seductions, playful withholding);

- special times (early mornings, afternoon);

- exhibitionism (dancing with/for partner, posing for imaginary photographs);

- using pet names for sexual body parts (Mr Big, Ms Pussy);

- talking 'dirty' (describing erotic activities or using profanities).

Many of the above have been included in the Sexual Fun Cards, which are similar to those you encountered in Session 5, 'Romance'. The Sexual Fun Cards are provided to help you kick-start your sexual fun and add a little 'spice' to your sex lives. Some people might find certain ideas and topics chosen for these cards too adventurous; others could find them too tame. The purpose of these cards is simply to offer a small variety of fun activities that are likely to appeal to as many people as possible. Couples with more specific or unusual preferences can add their own cards but should make sure these are acceptable to their partners.

Materials required

- Sexual Fun tables

- Scissors

- One small box with a lid

Instructions

The cards can be used whenever you and your partner have time alone together, without the usual interruptions of family, friends, television, etc.

1. Cut out the pages containing tables marked 'Sexual Fun Cards'.

2. Cut out each square in the tables to make your own cards and put them in your box.

   - Only remove those that you know you definitely do not want to try.

   - You might also wish to add some of your own, but remember to check with your partner to see if what you propose is acceptable.

3. Shake up the box, select one card each and choose one of the activities.

   - If a particular activity isn't possible at the time you select it, turn the card over and try the activity on the other side, or replace it in the box for later use and select another card.

Remember

 Sexual fun is about your mutual pleasure. Provided whatever you do is acceptable to both of you, there is no such thing as wrong, bad or silly.

From the Therapist's Chair

It is not possible to emphasise too strongly the importance of playfulness in a relationship. Sharing fun and laughter with a partner can keep a relationship fresh and exciting. Sexual fun and fantasy enables people to loosen their inhibitions and develop flexible sexual scenarios that can enhance their sex life, as well as strengthen their intimate bonds.

I have worked with couples of all ages, from diverse backgrounds and cultures, with nearly every problem imaginable. The success these couples have achieved in therapy has been because of their willingness to cooperate with each other and work together as an intimate team. Only when these couples reach the playful stage of their therapy, and I see the delight they bring to each other, am I confident that they have developed a safe and joyous context for the continued development of a healthy, resilient relationship.

Points to ponder

- Adults need play – it makes them and their relationships happy and healthy.

- Taking the time to replenish your relationship through play is one of the best things you can do for each other.

- Sexual play can help couples discover what is safe and dangerous, as well as establish boundaries within the relationship.

✂ SEXUAL FUN CARDS

Arm wrestling in your underwear; or, better yet, naked.	*Use a feather or furry mitten to caress your partner's body.*
Caress your partner's body using a vibrator.	*Using your hot mouth, arouse your partner's nipples or genitals, then put an ice cube in your mouth and cool down your overheated partner.*
Caress, kiss and lick your partner's vagina/penis.	*Wearing a blindfold, stroke your partner's body and try to identify from their reactions which areas they like being touched.*
Describe a fantasy that you think your partner would enjoy.	*Watch a sexy movie together.*
Caress, kiss or lick a place on your partner's body that you don't usually pay attention to.	*Describe how your partner's genitals feel while caressing them, using sexy language to heighten the erotic feelings.*
Cover your body with fruit and get your partner to eat healthily.	*Describe a setting (real or fantasy) in which you would like to have sex.*

Get dressed up as a character (e.g. nurse, fireman) that you think your partner would like.	Describe something that turns you on sexually.
Give your partner a full body massage with your feet.	Describe something that you like that is (i) hot, (ii) wet, (iii) slow and (iv) fast.
Give your partner a full body massage with your lips.	Discuss booking a 'dirty' weekend away, what you would take with you and do with each other.
Write your partner a sexy letter.	Tell your partner about a fantasy you have had about her/him.
Give your partner an orgasm using your hands.	Tell your partner what item of clothing you feel sexy in and explain why.
Give your partner an orgasm using your mouth.	Tell your partner what sexual risks you would like to take.

Next time you go out with your partner leave your underwear at home.

Touch your partner in a sensual way when you are not in bed.

Have a night when you wear whatever clothes your partner chooses.

Try a little fun bondage using ribbons.

Have a private photo shoot (real camera/film optional).

Undress your partner very slowly.

Have a shower or bath together.

Put on your sexiest underwear and dressing gown and tease your partner with 'quick flashes' of parts of your body.

Have an uninterrupted night of kissing and caressing and anything else you can think of but no penetrative sex.

Put some food (yoghurt, chocolate, honey, etc.) on the part of your body you want your partner to lick.

Have phone sex with your partner.

Take your partner's hands on a journey around your body.

Kiss your partner's body until you find the spot that they most enjoy.	*Perform a striptease for your partner.*
Leave your partner a voice recording of what you want to do when you are both alone.	*Place one hand over your partner's heart and notice how his/her heartbeat increases when you caress them in an erotic way.*
Tell without words (using mime, facial expression, gestures etc.) something sensual you would like your partner to do for you.	*Place your partner's hand on the part of your body you would most like to have touched.*
Make love in a room other than the bedroom.	*Play a game of strip poker or snap.*
Make love with all your clothes on	*Play naked blind man's buff.*
Meet your partner in a public place wearing nothing but your underwear and a long coat.	*Play out your partner's fantasy.*

Post therapy

No therapist has a magic wand or miracle potion at their disposal that will quickly fix your problems. Neither do therapists have all the answers, since people are individuals and each relationship is different from any other.

Working through any therapy programme requires a great deal of courage, commitment and motivation on the part of those involved. In face-to-face therapy, therapists offer individuals and couples support and guidance, as well as providing homework exercises to be undertaken between visits. For some couples, having a regularly scheduled appointment with a therapist and having to report back on the progress of their homework exercises can be a strong motivator. In DIY therapy, you and your partner have worked without the visits to a therapist. However, the underlying learning processes are similar; the one main difference is that *you* have been in control. In other words, you have worked at your own pace and you have found the best type of support and encouragement you can get – from each other. The bonds that you have forged will help you face any future problems together.

In this book you have been introduced to many of the communication and therapeutic techniques and exercises commonly used in face-to-face therapy. In addition, Sessions 5, 'Romance' and 10, 'Fun and fantasy' focused on rediscovering the passion in your relationship, which is frequently ignored in therapy.

We often think of having fun as trivial: it might not seem important, or even possible, when the troubles of your relationship (or the world) are weighing you down. But play serves a number of functions in life besides making us happy. It is as important to our physical and mental health as eating well and exercising, it helps us relieve stress, lifts our spirits and distracts us from the problems of life. Play supercharges learning, fosters creativity, develops flexibility and teaches us how to manage and transform our 'negative' emotions and experiences. It promotes bonding, develops compassion and heals resentments. Through regular play, partners learn to trust one another, enabling them to work together towards deeper levels of intimacy and try new experiences. Fun and excitement bring couples together and it is play that can help them stay together. When people say they want their relationship to be like it was in the beginning, what they are looking for are some of the pleasures and passions they experienced when they first met. Couples using the exercises in Sessions 5, 'Romance' and 10, 'Fun and fantasy' have discovered that not only are they able to rekindle the flames of romance and passion but also they are better equipped to deal with any future difficulties they might face.

Maintaining your relationship

Completing any kind of relationship therapy programme is not unlike getting your driving licence. Your driving instructor can teach you how to drive and keep you safe but, when the lessons are over, it is only continual 'practice' that will make you a good driver. Throughout your DIY therapy you have been provided with exercises and techniques to help you learn how to steer your relationship in the right direction, but you still need to continue to build on the work you have done to avoid slipping back into old habits. The way to ensure that new habits become second nature is practice, practice and more practice.

The final piece of work I ask couples to undertake is to draw up a relationship maintenance plan with regular service checks. Your plan should last for at least two months and include fun activities (like those in Session 5, 'Romance' and Session 10, 'Fun and fantasy') with weekly check-ups. While your check-ups can be used to discuss any difficulties you have, this is not their sole purpose. Psychological research has found that reminding ourselves of the good things in our lives and expressing gratitude can substantially increase our happiness levels. Therefore, in your weekly check-ups, you should limit your discussion time on problems to 20 minutes and spend the rest of the hour telling your partner: (a) what you have enjoyed about your week; (b) what you are grateful for; and (c) what you are looking forward to.

From the Therapist's Chair

At this point you might be wondering where love features in all of this. In this book I have deliberately avoided talking about love – simply because there are no methods or techniques that can make people fall in or out of love. Love is a highly complex emotion that has defied adequate scientific explanation. On this topic it is sufficient to say that if you have bought or borrowed this book, or are just flicking through it to see what it might offer, you obviously have enough love for your partner to want the best relationship you can have.

At the beginning of this book I said that the only experts in a relationship are those involved and that they are ultimately responsible for their own success in therapy. Consequently, with the right techniques and sufficient application, couples can resolve their own issues. My hope is that, in completing your DIY therapy programme, you have not simply resolved your problems but also found ways to rekindle romance, renew your sexual excitement and rediscover the joys of a truly intimate relationship.

Index